STUDIES IN LAW, POLITICS, AND SOCIETY

STUDIES IN LAW, POLITICS, AND SOCIETY

Series Editor: Austin Sarat

Recent volumes:

STUDIES IN LAW, POLITICS, AND SOCIETY

EDITED BY

AUSTIN SARAT

Department of Law, Jurisprudence & Social Thought and Political Science, Amherst College

Symposium: Hatred and the Law

United Kingdom – North America – Japan
India – Malaysia – China

Emerald Publishing Limited
Howard House, Wagon Lane, Bingley BD16 1WA, UK

First edition 2021

Copyright © 2021 Emerald Publishing Limited

Reprints and permissions service
Contact: permissions@emeraldinsight.com

British Library Cataloguing in Publication Data
A catalogue record for this book is available from the British Library

ISBN: 978-1-80071-221-8 (Print)
ISBN: 978-1-80071-220-1 (Online)
ISBN: 978-1-80071-222-5 (Epub)

ISSN: 1059-4337 (Series)

Printed and bound by CPI Group (UK) Ltd, Croydon, CR0 4YY

ISOQAR certified
Management System,
awarded to Emerald
for adherence to
Environmental
standard
ISO 14001:2004.

Certificate Number 1985
ISO 14001

INVESTOR IN PEOPLE

CONTENTS

LIST OF CONTRIBUTORS

Chara Bakalis	Oxford Brookes University, UK
Jeannine Bell	Indiana University, USA
Jeffrey R. Dudas	University of Connecticut, USA
Marian Duggan	University of Kent, UK
Julia Hornle	Queen Mary University of London, UK
Emma Ricknell	Linnaeus University, Sweden

EDITORIAL BOARD

SECTION I

GENERAL ARTICLE

CHAPTER 1

SAME PROCEDURE AS LAST YEAR? PATTERNS OF DEATH PENALTY BILL INTRODUCTIONS IN THE ERA OF ABOLITION 1999–2018

Emma Ricknell

ABSTRACT

The death penalty has existed in a state of steady decline for the last two decades, during which state legislatures have been at the center of abolition efforts. Successful abolition is, however, very rare in contrast to how often death penalty repeal bills are introduced across state legislatures, year after year. Indeed, abolition is not a sudden event, but may be many years in the making. Research on the early phases of this process, where the groundwork for enacted legislation is laid, is nevertheless limited. This chapter explores patterns of death penalty bill introductions across all active death penalty states from 1999 to 2018, providing not only an overview of legislative activity at state level but also an analysis of potential factors fueling the activity. It argues that individual legislators play a significant role in the current trend of increased legislative support for a restricted, if not entirely abolished, death penalty, evident both in terms of persistency over time and cooperation across party lines. It also problematizes partisan aspects of legislative activity in the context of legislation on capital punishment.

Keywords: Death penalty; bill introductions; state legislatures; legislative entrepreneurs; abolition; partisanship

Studies in Law, Politics, and Society, Volume 85, 3–26
Copyright © 2021 by Emerald Publishing Limited
All rights of reproduction in any form reserved
ISSN: 1059-4337/doi:10.1108/S1059-433720210000085001

INTRODUCTION

The death penalty has since the turn of the century existed in a state of "free-fall" (Steiker & Steiker, 2014). Executions and death sentences are at historically low levels (Death Penalty Information Center, 2019a), as is public support (Jones, 2019). With 10 states having abolished the death penalty during the new millennium and an additional three having a gubernatorial moratorium in place,[1] there is an expectation that remaining death penalty states will eventually follow suit, likely by legislative repeal (Entzeroth, 2012; Galliher, Koch, Keys, & Guess, 2002).

Abolition is, however, not a sudden event. Even if an abolition bill ends up successful, earlier versions very likely experienced rejection a number of times throughout the legislative process, much like with any legislation introduced in state legislatures (Squire & Moncrief, 2019). Yet considering the flurry of activity regarding the death penalty in recent years, we know surprisingly little about this early phase of the legislative process. What we do know, is that the legislative activity during the early phase of the legislative process reflects the overall trend of an on-going decline for the death penalty, as bills aiming to if not repeal, at least restrict the death penalty are today the most common type of death penalty bill (Baumgartner, Davidson, Johnson, Krishnamurthy, & Wilson, 2018). However, we have scant knowledge about the legislators behind this pattern across states and over time, and cannot say under which conditions those legislators introduced their bills in the first place. If the bill introduction phase, the necessary starting point for all policies decided by state legislatures, is at all indicative of future outcomes, it is high time pay it some attention.

The aim of this chapter is to begin to address this research gap. I do so by examining determinants of death penalty bill introductions over time and across states during the last two decades. Specifically, I examine the introduction of death penalty-related bills in all death penalty states for the years 1999–2018, using a unique dataset. My approach is based upon an understanding that not only is studying the early phases of the legislative process important for understanding current overall trends, but also a comprehensive approach that covers *all* bills relating to the policy as it facilitates a contrasting analysis relevant to the current state of decline that would otherwise not be possible.

As will be elaborated upon below, I draw primarily upon research on legislative entrepreneurs and partisan aspects concerning capital punishment to guide the analysis on patterns of bill introductions. This approach enables an analysis of patterns among legislators of individual leadership as well as bipartisan collaborations, and also the partisan context within which these legislative actions were taken.

This chapter, thus, adds to the limited number of studies that have used cross-sectional, time-series approaches to examine legislative activity in the area of capital punishment. It shows the impact of legislative entrepreneurship and party control of the legislature and governor's mansion on the number of bill introductions, depending on bill category, highlighting in particular the impact individual legislators have on current patterns of legislative activity.

UNDERSTANDING DEATH PENALTY LEGISLATION

Inherent in acting within an environment of various constraints, meaning here a state legislature, are decisions on how to spend one's limited resources. A basic starting point for viewing legislators spend these resources, for example, by introducing legislation that has very little chance of gaining any support, is that they are rational, goal-oriented actors that aim to optimize gains within the boundaries of established institutions (e.g. Schiller, 1995; Wawro, 2000). Their motivations might stem from goals of varying importance to themselves, such as preferences of what constitutes "good public policy," re-election prospects and gaining ground within the institution itself (Fenno, 1973). Translated into the context of capital punishment, patterns of bill introductions can, thus, be discussed both in terms of legislators' leadership, promoting policies that, for example, aim to eliminate the risk of wrongful executions, as well as strategic, individual career advancements, where decisions based upon the latter do not negate an attempt of developing a leadership position on a particular policy issue for a variety of other reasons. Indeed, legislators very likely pursue multiple goals (Fenno, 1973; Hall, 1996).

Beginning with the aspect of political leadership, it has indeed been a recurring theme in research seeking to explain legislators' decisions to support legislation aiming to restrict the death penalty. Researchers have pointed to the act of supporting legislation that aims to if not repeal, at least narrow a death penalty statute as requiring political courage (Kirchmeier, 2006), or a willingness to accept considerable political cost (Galliher et al., 2002), particularly when considering that the majority of voters have for decades been supportive of the death penalty (Jones, 2019). Abolition efforts, thus, likely involve those who can politically afford it, for example, withstand a charge of being "soft on crime" (Culver, 1999; Garland, 2010), and may include some form of political elite (Harcourt, 2008; Sarat, Malague, De los Santos, Pedersen, Qasim, Seymour, & Wishloff, 2019; Wozniak, 2012).

The importance of political leadership is supported by historical studies of abolition in the United States (Davis, 1957; Galliher, Ray, & Cook, 1992), as well as by numerous studies providing detailed insight into both successful and unsuccessful abolition efforts by state legislators and governors, for example, in California (Culver & Boyens, 2002), Colorado (Radelet, 2017), Illinois (Warden, 2012), Kansas (Galliher & Galliher, 1997), Maryland (Milleman, 2010), Michigan (Koch & Galliher, 1993), New Jersey (Henry, 2008; Martin, 2010; Wozniak, 2012), New Hampshire (Sarat, 2002), New Mexico (e.g. Entzeroth, 2012; Parker, 2013) and Oregon (Kaplan, 2013). Additionally, abolition in modern time has from a global perspective consistently occurred against the wishes of the public majority (Hood & Hoyle, 2015; Zimring & Hawkins, 1986); described as "leadership from the front" (Buxton, 1974, p. 245).

In situations as such, where legislators are working against the current, bills may require "champions" who invest considerable time and resources to promote and push the bills through the legislature. Entrepreneurship within legislatures have since long been theorized, yet to distinguish legislative entrepreneurship from activities that legislators engage in on a daily basis simply by performing their general duties, Wawro (2000) defines legislative entrepreneurship as a set of activities that a legislator engages in, which involves working to form coalitions of other members for the purpose of passing legislation by combining various legislative inputs and issues in order to affect legislative outcomes. (p. 4)

These activities, Wawro (2000) explains, can be distilled into four main areas: acquiring information, bill drafting, coalition building and pushing legislation (p. 5). Wozniak (2012) in turn highlights these types of activities in a study of efforts to abolish the death penalty in New Jersey and Maryland during the 2000s, finding that legislative entrepreneurs advocating for abolition were of particular importance in New Jersey, contributing to the state abolishing the death penalty in 2007.

Bill proposals aiming to restrict or abolish can, thus, from the lens of legislative entrepreneurship be seen as part of a long-term effort to achieve a legislative goal, with persistency, leadership and the ability to make coalitions with other legislators over time as important aspects. There are to the author's knowledge no equivalent examples of research concerning bills with the aim of preserving or expanding the death penalty, but the idea of legislative entrepreneurship applies to introductions of such bills as well.

Legislative entrepreneurs, however, act within an electoral context as well, which leads to a long-running theme in the literature on capital punishment. Over many decades, researchers have pointed to ideology as being an influential factor. Particularly relevant for the focus of this chapter, is the prior research on the connection between partisan affiliation and death penalty support or opposition.

On the one hand, there is support for a distinction between the two parties, with Republicans tending to be more supportive of the death penalty compared to Democrats. Scholars have over decades founds such patterns in studies involving both voters and elected officials (e.g. Baumer, Messner, & Rosenfeld, 2003; Galliher et al., 2002; Nice, 1992; Sarat, 2001; Steiker & Steiker, 2006; Vidmar & Ellsworth, 1974).

Avoiding to appear as "soft on crime," as referenced above, becomes further relevant here. Even though capital punishment was effectively suspended by the United States Supreme Court's decision in *Furman* v. *Georgia* in 1972, the decision allowed states to rewrite their statutes to pass constitutional muster. Within 5 years, 35 states had done exactly so (Steiker & Steiker, 2014). This development is part of a much larger context of punitive penal policy developments originating around this time period (see e.g. McCann & Johnson, 2009, pp. 147–153), and unsurprisingly, the majority of citizens have since the mid-1970s supported the use of the death penalty (Jones, 2019; Masci, 2017). Starting from the early 1970s to the early 1990s, capital punishment gained a very prominent role among Republicans and was transformed into a symbol that could represent a punitive attitude toward law and order as a whole, functioning as a "wedge issue" separating the two parties and ultimately benefiting the Republicans (Garland, 2010, p. 247). A politicized issue as such can, thus, be is used as a sort of tool in the strategic pursuit of publicity and to advance one's career (Dingerson, 1991; Garland, 2010; Steiker, 2002, 2012). Indeed, research points to the likelihood of a state having a death penalty law in the first place to be greater when Republicans occupy at least 60% of the seats in the legislature (Jacobs & Carmichael, 2002).

An important ingredient in how a tough stance of capital punishment can be capitalized upon politically, however, applies not just to state legislators. The entire criminal justice system is closely related to electoral politics. That means that if expressing opposition or even doubt regarding capital punishment, means you can risk being seen as not being for law and order as a whole, this applies to a wide range of public officials, who are directly elected in the United States to a far greater extent than, for example, in Europe. This includes officials explicitly involved in the administration of the death penalty, beyond politicians, such as judges, prosecutors and police chiefs (Bae, 2007; Garland, 2010; Sarat et al., 2019).

On the other hand, the partisan division described above comes with caveats. While research has found a pattern of Republican endorsement of capital punishment in a general sense, the partisan division falters if Democratic opposition is not convincing. Part of the gains the Republican Party made in taking charge of the "law and order" approach in the 1970s was after all built upon securing the Southern white vote – a group of voters which had voted solidly in favor of the Democratic Party since the Civil War (Garland, 2010). Furthermore, while the function of capital punishment as a wedge that could split both parties into two sides of the entire debate on criminal justice did develop, by the mid-1990s it had begun to transform at the national level (Holian, 2004). In 1992, the Democratic candidate for president (then-Governor Bill Clinton) famously interrupted his campaign to oversee the execution of a brain-damaged man, Ricky Ray Rector (Soss, Langbein, & Metelko, 2003). Two years later, President Clinton signed the Violent Crime Control and Law Enforcement Act after its passage in the Democratic-controlled Congress, written largely by the chairman of the Senate Judiciary Committee, Democratic Senator Joe Biden. This very comprehensive crime bill included the Federal Death Penalty Act, which vastly expanded the number of death-eligible federal crimes by 60 in total. In 1996, President Clinton signed the Antiterrorism and Effective Death Penalty Act (AEDPA) after it too had received bipartisan support in a now Republican-controlled Congress, an act that severely limited the ability for death row inmates to seek relief in federal court for errors and abuses at state level (Williams, 2012). The generally clear divide between the two parties now became blurred on the issue of capital punishment (Garland, 2010).

Thus, while Republican enthusiasm for the death penalty may have been easy to spot during previous decades, such a finding can obscure the fact that over time, Democratic opposition may not have been equally evident (Bae, 2007), and should not be seen as a guarantee (Wozniak, 2012). Even when it comes to the Republican Party, positions have fluctuated historically (Jones, 2018). Considering the two most recent decades and the decline of the death penalty, a simple partisan explanation does not rhyme well with the composition of state legislatures, since they have predominantly either been split between the two parties, or been under Republican control (National Conference on State Legislatures, 2020). Alternatively, while effects for party on death penalty opinion have been shown, the effects may simply be too modest to be part of the main story (Soss et al., 2003).

EXPECTATIONS

Previous studies on death penalty legislation find different conclusions regarding the importance of political leadership and partisanship, and the overall motivations to why legislators engage in the promotion of legislation concerning capital punishment. Considering, however, that legislators act based upon multiple, not necessarily competing motivations, the aim here is not to dismiss any particular theory. Elucidating exact motivations of individual legislators over time across multiple states also comes with considerable methodological difficulty. As this chapter focuses on overall patterns of legislative activity, it treats the different explanations presented above as complimentary. However, there are expectations pertaining to differences when it comes to the two main categories of bills examined, that is, bills aiming to promote the continued use of the death penalty, or even expand it, and bills aiming to do the opposite, that is, restrict or even abolish altogether.

First, I expect legislative entrepreneurs to have an effect on the level of activity when it comes to bill introductions. This applies to both categories of bills, as there is no theoretical basis for assuming that only one category is relevant for examination. However, as leadership is part of the analysis, it is logical to expect that a difference in activity for bill introductions that in different ways challenge the existence of the death penalty altogether, as opposed to those that do not. Therefore, while I legislative entrepreneurs to have a positive effect on the number of bill introductions in general, such effects are expected to be greater when it comes to restrictive bills.

Second, despite the mixed results regarding the role of party in the context of death penalty legislation, I expect an effect on the activity levels by legislators when it comes to bill introductions. Specifically, I expect a Republican majority in the chambers of the legislature, as well as a Republican governor, to have a negative effect on activity, based upon the general division between Republicans and Democrats where the former to a greater extent promotes the continued use of the death penalty.

MODEL SPECIFICATION, DATA AND METHOD

This study examines determinants of introductions of death penalty-related bills in the 38 states which had a death penalty statute at some point during the years 1999–2018. The unit of analysis is state-years and the dependent variable is the number of death penalty-related bill introductions. The variation in activity between states is considerable. In some states, there is constant activity every year, while in others, perhaps only one or two bills are introduced, if any at all. The data, thus, have a high incidence of zero, or very few counts. As is appropriate for modeling count data that exhibits over-dispersion in the dependent variable, meaning the variance is larger than the mean, I use maximum likelihood negative binomial regression (Long, 1997).[2] I control for year and state-fixed effects to capture constant differences across states, and account for heteroscedasticity and serial dependency by estimating standard errors clustered by a variable composed of the intersection of state and year.

Dependent Variable

To capture and examine predictors of bill introductions in the context of death penalty legislation, introduced bills were collected from each state's official state legislature website.[3] Regarding the chosen time period 1999–2018, the starting year has previously been identified as a watershed year, being the year when bills supporting the continued use of the death penalty ceased to be the most common (Baumgartner et al., 2018). The study, thus, covers the beginning of the decline of the death penalty. A number of additional choices regarding the collection of data were furthermore made during the process.

First, this study comprises *introduced* legislation as opposed to *enacted*. Certainly, enacted bills provide the obvious source for tracking and analyzing the way policies develop over time. Yet the multi-step process of enacting a bill is not identical to the step of introducing a bill (Karch, 2007). If research comprises only bills that become law, a significant part of legislative decision-making is neglected. Looking at the much larger collection of introduced bills (over 3,400) in contrast to how many of those became law (421), the latter only provides a limited view of how frequently legislators try to amend their state's respective death penalty statute. Arguably, factors predicting high activity in one category of bills could predict legislative success for those bills over time, as highly controversial and complex legislation processes have to start somewhere.

A second choice regarding data collection pertains to the content of the bills. The criterion for including a bill is more inclusive than the bill being one that exclusively pertains to the death penalty. For instance, a bill aiming to reform the appeals process may affect more than just capital defendants. Yet to be included, a bill text explicitly has to state consequences for capital defendants, meaning broader, non-specific or omnibus criminal justice bill proposals are not part of the collected data.

Lastly, when it comes to the coding of the direction of individual bills, the division between the two categories restrictive and supportive bills is based upon their intended purpose. The basic idea is that the former category contains legislation with the ultimate aim of limiting, if not removing altogether, the number of death sentences and executions, while the latter aims to facilitate if not more, but the continued existence of such. For details regarding the coding of the dependent variable, see Appendix 1.

Primary Independent Variables

Quantifying legislative entrepreneurship comes with great difficulty (Wawro, 2000). With a dependent variable consisting of a count of introduced bills, the acts of individual legislators become less clear, in return for an analysis of overall patterns. However, the sponsorship of each bill proposal has been coded and based upon these data two distinct aspects of legislative entrepreneurship have been operationalized. First, a variable that tracks the existence of individual legislators, or a cohesive group of legislators, being *particularly active* in terms of bill introductions, thus, having a disproportionate effect on the dependent variable. First, the variable tracks the annual proportion of the total number of bills introduced by one individual legislator or cohesive group of legislator when that individual or group sponsor at least three bills. Second, it tracks the proportion of bills introduced by legislators who only introduce one bill one year, yet introduce the same or similar bill over multiple years; the cut-off being at least three years during the studied time period to be included. This variable aims to capture the activities of legislative entrepreneurs when it comes to their tenacity in information gathering and bill drafting. The resulting variable is one that shows the percentage of the total number of bills introduced by such a legislator or group of legislators.

The second variable aiming to capture legislative entrepreneurship tracks coalition building operationalized by the existence of bipartisan bills introduced in a year in each state, expressed in percentages of the total annual count.[4] No distinction is made in the data between primary sponsors and co-sponsors, as this distinction varies across state legislatures in terms of importance and function (Holman & Mahoney, 2019). The alternative measure, that is, one based upon primary sponsorship, is furthermore not necessarily more accurate, as the primary sponsor may not be the actual original author (Wawro, 2000). Even though a draft of a bill was, for example, authored by an interest group, or is essentially a copy of a previous bill authored by another legislator, its introduction nevertheless adds to the aggregated pattern of activity, as analysis of individual legislators is of primary focus here. Higher rates of *bipartisan sponsorship* could indicate greater coalition building in the legislature. Together, these two variables, thus, represent aspects that relate to the four main types of activities Wawro (2000) identifies that legislative entrepreneurs engage in, that is, acquiring information, bill drafting, coalition building and pushing legislation.

A second set of primary independent variables controls for party control of the legislature. Party is expected to have an effect on legislative activity depending on bill category, despite the mixed results of partisanship in previous research described above. Partisanship is represented by two dummy variables indicating *Republican control of the state house and senate* each year, respectively.[5] A dummy variable for *Republican governor* is also added.

State Institutional Context and Control Variables

Examining data which consist of a count of bills require consideration of the highly varying institutional context those bills were presented within. To begin with, the level of legislative professionalism has been shown to have broad consequences for the policy process (e.g. Squire, 1992, 2007; Squire & Moncrief, 2019), including legislative output (Squire, 1998). It also relates to the actual policy decisions legislators make, with professionalized legislatures being more inclined to introduce legislation intended to reform government practices, as well as to adopt more complex regulatory policies, having more time and resources in legislative sessions to evaluate and ultimately vote on bills (Squire & Moncrief, 2019). This may result in a promotion of more progressive policies on controversial issues (Lax & Phillips, 2009). A previous study encompassing all US states also shows that states with higher levels of professionalization are less likely to have the death penalty (Gerber, 1999). Squire's index of *legislative professionalism*, an index which compares salary, staff and time-in-session of each state legislature to that of the US Congress (Squire, 2012, 2017), is included to account for this aspect. Term limits have, however, been found to not only reduce the effects of professionalization

(Kousser, 2005) and naturally, increase turnover (Squire & Moncrief, 2019) but also to encourage lawmakers to pursue legislation that renders quick political benefits (Cain & Kousser, 2004), all of which may affect legislative activity. I, thus, also control for the existence of *term limits* (13 legislatures in the dataset) by adding a dummy variable.

A number of indicators related to the administration of the death penalty are furthermore added. The practical administration of the death penalty in a state, most explicitly via the annual number of new *death sentences*, as well as the number of *executions*, could send signals to legislators that would have an effect on their actions in the legislature. As the death penalty started declining toward the end of the 1990s, this pattern started to appear in multiple places yet at varying pace. In some states, there was very little movement at all for such indicators, such as in New Hampshire, as levels were already at a minimum. Moreover, a connection between capital punishment and homicide rates has since long been debated and studied, the main question being whether the death penalty can function as a deterrent (Radelet & Lacock, 2009). The results that pertain specifically to legislative activity are, however, very mixed. Some show a connection with homicide rates and the enactment of death penalty statutes in the states (Langer & Brace, 2005; Nice, 1992), while others do not (Galliher et al., 2002). Other, country-level studies show a relationship between higher crime rates and a higher likelihood of abolition (Kent, 2010), as well as no significant relationship with abolition (Ruddell & Urbina, 2004). With this uncertainty in mind, a variable controlling for the annual *state homicide rate* is included.

Finally, I also control for two aspects relating to overall bill production in the states. The first consists of the *total number of bills* introduced annually in each legislature, a number that varies greatly between the states but remains relatively stable within the states. Second, I add a dummy variable to account for *biannual sessions*, pertaining to the four state legislatures (Montana, Nevada, Oregon (until 2009) and Texas) of the total 38 which do not meet every year but biannually in odd years, meaning their count of bill introductions is zero during non-session years. Summary descriptive statistics along with sources and coding of all variables are available in Appendices 2 and 3, respectively.

GENERAL PATTERNS OF LEGISLATIVE ACTIVITY

Before launching into the full analysis, I first present visualizations of the data that illustrate general patterns. A significant amount of variation is expected, as annual bill introduction totals for states in a general sense can vary from a few hundred in a state like Wyoming, to tens of thousands in a state like New York (Squire & Moncrief, 2019). Looking, however, at the aggregate, the general pattern is in line with previous findings by Baumgartner et al. (2018) regarding bill introductions during the two most recent decades of death penalty decline, with restrictive bills being more common than supportive (2,057 vs 1,348). Fig. 1 sorts all states by the total number of restrictive bill introductions, and shows the great range of activity across the states during the studied time period. Among

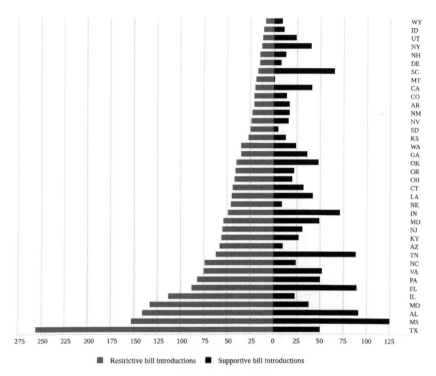

WY
ID
UT
NY
NH
DE
SC
MT
CA
CO
AR
NM
NV
SD
KS
WA
GA
OK
OR
OH
CT
LA
NE
IN
MD
NJ
KY
AZ
TN
NC
VA
PA
FL
IL
MO
AL
MS
TX

275   250   225   200   175   150   125   100   75   50   25   0   25   50   75   100   125

■ Restrictive bill introductions   ■ Supportive bill introductions

Fig. 1.   Total Bill Introductions (Supportive and Restrictive) by State 1999–2018.
Note: States sorted by restrictive bill introduction totals.

retentionist states, the lopsided totals of South Carolina's legislature in favor
of supportive bill introductions stand out, while a number of states display the
opposite lopsided totals, for example, Montana and Arizona. The very active legislature in Texas represents a significant proportion of the sum of restrictive bills,
with Mississippi and Alabama trailing behind. As bill introduction totals can,
however, be the result of unique events during individual years, such as special
sessions, an illustration of averages over time can provide further clarification.

Fig. 2 is a choropleth map of bill categorical leaning of each state during 1999–
2018, a visual rendering of the *average* activity state regarding the two categories
of bills. Calculating averages, thus, removes the potential impact of outlier years.[6]
The overall pattern in the map provides further illustration of the trend of restrictive bills being on average more commonly introduced compared to supportive
bills. Only 10 states introduce on average more supportive bills throughout the
studied time period, with states such as Georgia and Idaho only slightly leaning toward supportive bills. The map also shows that the very large number of
restrictive bill introductions when it comes to Texas, is not the result of an outlier
session, but is instead a very consistent pattern in the state. Likewise, even though
the totals are radically different, both Montana and Arizona lean on average
very convincingly toward restrictive bills. South Carolina is correspondingly very
persistent in introducing supportive bills over time.

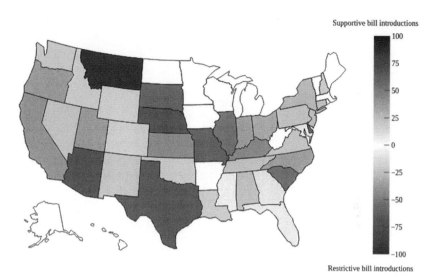

Fig. 2. Average Annual Trend for Bill Introductions (Supportive and Restrictive) by State 1999–2018. *Notes*: States in grayscale (values above 0): on and average, bills supporting the death penalty are more common in a year by a proportion ranging from 0 to 100. States in red scale (values below 0): on and average, bills restricting the death penalty are more common in a year by a proportion ranging from 0 to −100. For example, in the state of Montana, restrictive bills on an average represent 97% more of bill introductions compared to supportive bills. In contrast, in South Carolina, supportive bills are proportionally far more common (55%) than restrictive. States in white represent non-death penalty states.

Many of the restrictive bills part of the above totals have come in response to a number of landmark US Supreme Court decisions in the 2000s, for example, *Atkins* v. *Virginia* (2002) (declaring that the execution of the mentally retarded is unconstitutional), *Roper* v. *Simmons* (2005) (declaring that the execution of juveniles is unconstitutional) and *Kennedy* v. *Louisiana* (2008) (declaring that it is unconstitutional to impose the death penalty for the crime of raping a child, when the victim does not die and death was not intended). Legislators have also attempted to affect death penalty trials and their subsequent appeals process through legislation, for example, by ensuring capital defendants have access to DNA testing and are sufficiently represented by competent and properly funded defense attorneys. Here, state legislatures have also had to act following a Supreme Court decision, that is, most importantly *Ring* v. *Arizona* (2002) (declaring that the decision to execute a defendant must be made by a jury, not a judge alone).

RESULTS OF COUNT MODELS

Table 1 presents the results of the negative binomial regressions of introduced death penalty bills in 38 states 1999–2018. Models 1 and 2 present coefficient values for each independent variable on the number of bills introduced in the

Table 1. Negative Binomial Regression of Annual Bill Introduction Totals 1999–2018.

Independent Variables	Model 1	Model 2
	Restrictive	Supportive
Active legislator(s) (%)	1.297***	0.870***
	(0.138)	(0.180)
Bipartisan sponsorship (%)	0.858***	1.103***
	(0.126)	(0.138)
Republican house (1 = yes)	0.348***	0.288*
	(0.134)	(0.159)
Republican senate (1 = yes)	−0.245*	0.0933
	(0.126)	(0.163)
Republican governor (1 = yes)	−0.0334	−0.00527
	(0.0829)	(0.109)
Legislative professionalism	0.122	2.974*
	(1.722)	(1.725)
Term limits (1 = yes)	−0.211	−0.262
	(0.182)	(0.196)
Death sentences	−0.0145	0.0256**
	(0.00955)	(0.0124)
Executions	0.00289	−0.0253
	(0.0137)	(0.0229)
State homicide rate	0.0566	0.00505
	(0.0418)	(0.0561)
Biennial session (1 = yes)	−0.626**	−0.143
	(0.286)	(0.322)
Total no. of bills (100s)	0.0241***	0.0155***
	(0.00382)	(0.00334)
Constant	0.466	0.959*
	(0.433)	(0.542)
Overdispersion (ln[alpha])	−1.517***	−1.123***
	(0.212)	(0.140)
Pseudo R^2	0.220	0.192
Observations	709	709

Note: Year and state fixed effects included (not reported). Standard errors clustered on state-year.
*** $p<0.01$, ** $p<0.05$, and * $p<0.1$.

category of restrictive and supportive, respectively. The results confirm that the data are modeled appropriately using negative binomial regression models, as the overdispersion parameter is significantly greater than zero (Hilbe, 2011).

Beginning with the variables aiming to capture legislative entrepreneurship, they each significantly predict the count of bill proposals of both category, yet with slightly varying strength. Legislators, acting either alone or as a group, have a much bigger impact on the number of restrictive bills. Examples of legislators behind such a pattern include Alabama Senator Henry "Hank" Sanders, a Democrat, solely responsible for introducing over 80 bills since the year 2000 along with groups such as a bipartisan group of senators in Pennsylvania headed by Republican Senator Edward Helfrick, involved in six out of eight restrictive bills introduced in that state in 1999.[7] In states which abolished the death penalty during the studied time period, two "champions" stand out above the rest: Democratic House Representative Gail Chasey of New Mexico and Democratic Senator Ernie Chambers of Nebraska. They both have remarkably consistent records of introducing restrictive bills, including the successful repeal bills in each state (2009 and 2015, respectively, noting that Nebraska's was later rejected in a referendum in 2016). Among the most active legislators behind high counts of supportive bills is, for example, Republican House Representative John L. Moore of Mississippi, who was solely responsible or co-sponsor of 36 bills with the aim of expanding the death penalty in his state during the years 2003–2016.

The results also show that the effect of bipartisanship is an important factor in terms of understanding patterns of bill introductions. While coalitions across the partisan isle that result in bipartisan bills, thus, have a positive impact when it comes to bills aiming to restrict the death penalty, the effect is contrary to expectations somewhat stronger for the supportive bill category. The bipartisan groups of legislators affecting the results consist of a number of committees, which are, with few exceptions, bipartisan by default (bipartisan defined at 20% representation by the opposing party), along with non-committee bipartisan groups of legislators introducing bills. State judiciary committees that were particularly active during the studied time when it came to introducing restrictive bills were located in states such as Connecticut, Florida, Kansas, Nevada, and for supportive bills in Connecticut, Florida, Idaho and Kansas. Non-committee bipartisan restrictive bill introductions were common over time in states such as Pennsylvania, Illinois and Delaware, and in Maryland, Oklahoma and Pennsylvania for supportive bills.

While the results in Table 1 show that there are differences in effects on bill counts based upon bill category when it comes to active legislators and coalition building in the form of bipartisan sponsoring, further interpretations of these variables are less straightforward. Interpretation can be facilitated by plotting the average marginal effects of the variables, showing the effect of a unit change in the independent variable upon the outcome variable. Figs. 3 and 4 plot the average marginal effect for each of the two variables respectively (with 95% confidence intervals), but importantly also displays the effects over time.

Beginning with Fig. 3, the greater impact active legislators have on the count of restrictive bills is visible, yet the effect on both categories of bills changes over time. Toward the end of the time period, the number of retentionist states has shrunk from 38 to 31, and at that point, the results indicate that the effect by active legislators has remained somewhat stable when it comes to restrictive bills, while the effect on the number of supportive bills is in a declining trend. Moving to Fig. 4, which plots the marginal effects of bipartisan sponsorship, a similar pattern appears, albeit with slightly less statistical certainty.

An overall interpretation of the results hints toward, on the one hand, less impact on bill introductions over time by legislators who are very active in introducing bills that aim to support the continued use of the death penalty. On the other hand, the results indicate less impact on bill introductions over time when it comes to coalition building across partisan lines for such supportive bills, meaning bills aiming to support the continued use among still retentionist states is a more polarizing issue toward the end of the studied time period.

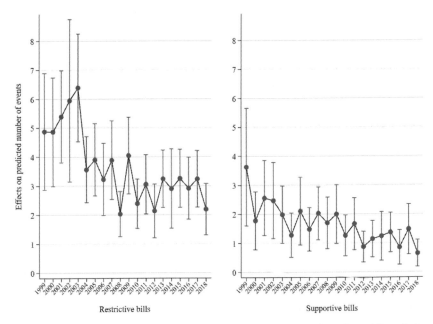

Fig. 3. Average Marginal Effects of Active Legislators on the Number of Restrictive and Supportive Bills, Respectively, 1999–2018.

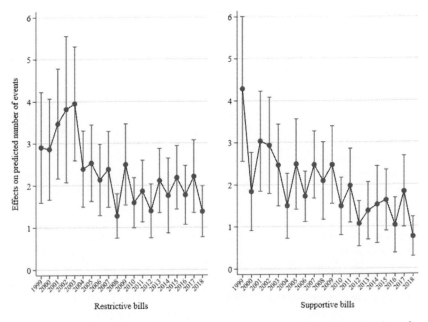

Fig. 4. Average Marginal Effects of Bipartisan Sponsorship on the Number of Restrictive and Supportive Bills, Respectively, 1999–2018.

Returning to the results in Table 1 and aspects of party control of the chambers and the governorship, the results are very similar for both models. A Republican-controlled house, contrary to the expectation put forth in this chapter, positively affects the number of restrictive bills, not only supportive bills. Holding all other variables constant, the results show that Republican-controlled house, is 41.6% more productive when it comes to restrictive bills, and 33.4% productive when it comes to supportive bills, compared to a Democratic-controlled house. As discussed above, the partisan effect should be anticipated with caution, and the results confirm that such caution is warranted. It is also possible that this finding is indicative of the incentive death penalty legislation provides for legislators in terms of positioning, meaning the drafting and introduction of bills that have no real chance of becoming law, but serve a purpose for the career purposes. Regarding party control of the senate, the results are, however, in line with expectations regarding the senate and restrictive bills. Holding all other variables constant, the results indicate a 21.7% drop in production compared to a senate controlled by a Democratic majority, while no corresponding statistically significant effect exists for supportive bills. When it comes to the governor, there is no statistically significant effect in either model.

For the remaining indicators, institutional aspects pertaining to legislative professionalism and term limits show mixed results, with the former having a positive effect on the count of bill introductions, but only for supportive bill introductions, the latter not having any significant effect in either model. Of the two variables that relate to the administration of the death penalty, only the number of death sentences indicates a statistically significant yet modest effect on the total count of supportive bills, a result in line with the idea that such numbers send signals to legislators that they potentially have in mind while proposing bills in either category. It is possible that this finding relates to the salience of the issue of capital punishment in a state, where the occurrence of death sentences, far more common compared to executions, can stir public interest in the issue throughout a year, and possibly also legislative interest. The annual state homicide rate has no effect on the count of bill introductions.

As a final effort to examine the patterns of legislative activity in the current state of death penalty decline, a comparison can be made between states where the legislature has successfully repealed the state's death penalty statute, and those where the legislature has not. Fig. 5 shows the results of such a separation based on the modeling done in Model 1 for restrictive bills, displaying the estimated coefficients for the variables pertaining to legislative entrepreneurs and partisanship.[8]

The results indicate that when it comes to legislative entrepreneurs, active individual legislators or groups of legislators constitute a main driving force in the introduction of bills in both groups of states, as also shown in Table 1. Bipartisan sponsorship is, however, not statistically significant in states that have legislatively abolished the death penalty, possibly providing indication that bipartisan coalitions are less likely to have an impact on legislative activity as a state leans toward abolition.

When it comes to partisan control of the state legislature, the overall pattern largely mirrors the results in Table 1, yet the relatively small number of abolitionist states and subsequently wide standard errors render a comparison between the two groups of states untenable. Separate modeling of the two groups of states, however,

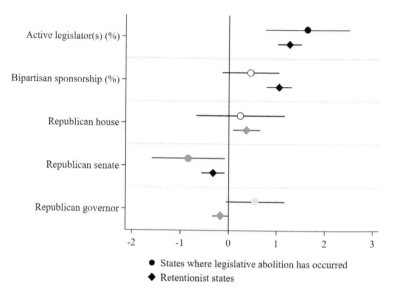

Fig. 5. Selected Estimated Coefficients in States Where Legislative Repeal has Occurred and in Retentionist States, 1999–2018 (Restrictive Bill Introductions Only). *Note*: Points represent the effect for each variable. Lines represent a 95% confidence interval. Points in black (circles and diamonds) are significantly different from zero at the 0.01 level, gray at 0.05 level, light gray at 0.1 level and hollow symbols not significantly different from zero at 0.1 level. The states included in the first category (states that have legislatively abolished): Colorado, Connecticut, Illinois, Maryland, Nebraska, New Hampshire, New Jersey and New Mexico. $N = 122$, Pseudo R^2: 0.215. For the other category (states which have not legislatively abolished), $N = 540$, Pseudo R^2: 0.265. Three states where the death penalty was declared unconstitutional during 1999–2018 omitted (Delaware, New York and Washington).

does reveal a result when it comes to partisan control of the governor's mansion. Having a Republican governor has a limited yet positive effect in abolitionist states, a result in need of further explanation. Two of the state legislatures that voted to abolish the death penalty during 1999–2018, Nebraska and New Hampshire, did indeed do so with a Republican behind the governor's desk. However, the Republican governors were hardly encouraging of the actions of the two legislatures, as the repeal bills were both met with gubernatorial vetoes, eventually both overridden. Nevertheless, the annual count of bills comprise far more restrictive bills than just abolition bills, meaning that a Republican governor should at least not by default be expected to have a negative effect on legislative activity for restrictive bills.

CONCLUSION

State legislators have continued to tinker with the death penalty since the turn of the millennium. It is likely that one of the repeal bills introduced this year in one of the remaining retentionist states will eventually lead to another state abolishing the death penalty. The results presented in this chapter provide further evidence to the ongoing development toward a more limited use of the death penalty in the United States, with the overall activity at the early stages of the legislative process pointing toward consistent activity in support of more restrictive policies. In absolute numbers, bill introductions of the opposite category, aiming toward the continued use of the death penalty, are becoming less common. This chapter shows that this trend can in part be explained by changes over time when it comes to bill introductions by particularly active legislators or groups of legislators, whose bills together with those of bipartisan groups of legislators are becoming less of an engine behind total counts of supportive bills. The display of political leadership, whether individually or in groups, is from this perspective more consistent over time among legislators preferring a more narrow death penalty, if one at all. Under Democratic control in the legislature, at least when it comes to the senate, it is furthermore likely that activity along these patterns continues.

Nevertheless, when it comes to partisanship, consider a recent repeal attempt. In early 2018, a death penalty repeal bill was introduced in the Washington State Legislature. Both chambers had a record of introducing repeal bills, making this the 15th one since 2005. In terms of party control, the Democrats had recently regained majority of the Senate, meaning the party now controlled both chambers. A Republican governor had not been elected in the state for decades, and a gubernatorial moratorium on executions had been imposed 4 years prior. None of the previous repeal bills had ever made it past the committee stage, but this time, upon being introduced in the Senate by request of the Attorney General, the bipartisan bill passed not only the Senate committee but also the Senate floor. However, after arriving in the House, it died (Wasserman, 2018). In October 2018, the Washington State Supreme Court nevertheless ruled that the current death penalty statute was unconstitutional, effectively abolishing the death penalty (La Corte & Johnson, 2018). Two consecutive attempts to formally remove the death penalty from the state's statute books have since failed in the legislature (Death Penalty Information Center, 2020).

Regarding aspects highlighted in this chapter, Washington exhibits a clear pattern of a number of persistent primarily Democratic legislators introducing restrictive bills while bipartisan sponsorship is less common. On an average, as shown in Fig. 2, the state tends to lean toward restrictive policies based upon bill introductions. Yet while legislative activity when it comes to restrictive bills can be explained to some extent by the claims regarding the importance of legislative entrepreneurs put forth in this chapter, the effects of partisanship remain difficult to predict. While previous research is indeed mixed, I would argue it nevertheless more often than not would predict abolition with such favorable conditions as a Democratic trifecta in place, as well as a number of other circumstances as mentioned above.

With this in mind, it is clear that to understand legislators' activity surrounding legislation aiming to restrict or repeal the death penalty, a broad approach is warranted. Future research could benefit from looking deeper into internal leadership aspects such as in committees and senior party members, contextual state-level factors such as demographics, along with other institutional and procedural state features potentially affecting the level of legislative activity in terms of bill introductions. Switching the unit of analysis to the legislators themselves instead of bills can also enable an examination of factors beyond party affiliation.

Additionally, the ascent of an "innocence frame" in the public debate relating to the death penalty since the end of the 1990s has been argued to be an important contributing factor to the decline of the death penalty (Baumgartner, De Boef, & Boydstun, 2008; Sarat, 2002). Qualitatively examining legislative activity, bill content and subsequent debates in the legislatures in relation to an ongoing media focus on wrongful convictions, such as by Wozniak (2012), can further enhance the analysis.

NOTES

1. New Jersey (2007), New York (2007), New Mexico (2009), Illinois (2011), Connecticut (2012), Maryland (2013), Delaware (2016), Washington (2018), New Hampshire (2019) and Colorado (2020). In New York, Delaware and Washington, the death penalty was declared unconstitutional, whereas abolition occurred legislatively in remaining states. The Nebraska legislature voted to repeal the death penalty in 2015, the year after it was, however, reinstated by public vote. Gubernatorial moratoriums are in place in Oregon (2011), Pennsylvania (2015) and California (2019). As of March 2020, there are 28 death penalty states.

2. The Stata command *nbreg* is applied in the statistical models. Although I have panel data and the command *xtnbreg* is available, adding fixed effects for year and state causes significant problems for models to converge. Additionally, *xtnbreg* has been found to be a problematic command for fixed effects modeling as it does not control for time-invariant variables. An alternative is, therefore, to use *nbreg* with dummies for year and state to represent the fixed effects (Allison & Waterman, 2002). The final model is *nbreg DV IVs i.year i.state, cluster (stateyear)*.

3. While the Lexis-Nexis State Legislative Universe database contains all bills introduced in US states, I chose to approach the original sources of the material directly to obtain the most comprehensive collection. States vary greatly when it comes to aspects such as formatting and categorization of bills, and my claim is that a collection process closer to the original source increases the probability for obtaining the most complete dataset.

4. This percentage includes bills introduced by committees, a very common practice in some states and by default means a bill is introduced on bipartisan grounds. My claim is that including such bills does not negate coalition building.

5. Nebraska's unique, unicameral, non-partisan legislature typically means the state is excluded from analyses involving partisanship. However, legislators in Nebraska *are* affiliated with one of the two major parties, information that is frequently referred to by, for example, newspapers, and this non-partisan legislature can indeed be said to exist within a very partisan context (Wright & Schaffner, 2002). The Nebraska Blue Books, provided by the legislature itself, furthermore list party affiliation of each current senator. This information has, therefore, been collected by the author and treated as affiliation equal to that of legislators in other states.

6. The calculation is based upon which category of bills is trending each year, divided by the total number of years. For example, if there are equal amounts of bills from each category proposed in a year, the score for that year is 0. If the total is three restrictive bills and five supportive bills one year, the latter category is trending by 25% (2/8) based upon how many more bills are introduced by that category out of the total number of bills. Years with no bills not included in average.

7. Interaction effects between the two variables aiming to capture legislative entrepreneurship have been modeled, but are not statistically significant.

8. A general issue when analyzing data involving death penalty abolition is the rarity of the event. The results in Fig. 5, thus, need to be analyzed with caution, and are discussed with this aspect in mind.

REFERENCES

Allison, P. D., & Waterman, R. (2002). Fixed effects negative binomial regression models. *Sociological Methodology, 32*(1), 247–265.

Baumer, E. P., Messner, S. F., & Rosenfeld, R. (2003). Explaining spatial variation in support for capital punishment: A multilevel analysis. *American Journal of Sociology, 104*(4), 844–875. doi:10.1086/367921

Bae, S. (2007). *When the state no longer kills: International human rights norms and abolition of capital punishment.* Albany, NY: State University of New York Press.

Baumgartner, F. R., De Boef, S. L., & Boydstun, A. E. (2008). *The decline of the death penalty and the discovery of innocence.* New York, NY: Cambridge University Press.

Baumgartner, F. R., Davidson M., Johnson K., Krishnamurthy A., & Wilson, C. (2018). *Deadly justice: A statistical portrait of the death penalty.* New York, NY: Oxford University Press.

Buxton, R. (1974). The politics of criminal law reform: England. *American Journal of Comparative Law, 25,* 244–256.

Cain, B. E., & Kousser, T. (2004). Adapting to term limits: Recent experiences and new directions. Retrieved from https://www.ppic.org/publication/adapting-to-term-limits-recent-experiences-and-new-directions

Culver, J. H. (1999). Capital punishment politics and policies in the states, 1977–1997. *Crime, Law & Social Change, 32,* 287–300. doi:10.1023/A:1008340620824

Culver, J. H., & Boyens, C. (2002). Political cycles of life and death: Capital punishment as public policy in California. *Albany Law Review, 65,* 991–1015.

Council of State Governments. (Various years). *The book of the states.* Lexington, KY: Council of State Governments. Retrieved from http://knowledgecenter.csg.org/kc/category/content-type/content-type/book-states

Davis, D. B. (1957). The movement to abolish capital punishment in America, 1787–1861. *American Historical Review, 63,* 23–46. doi:10.2307/1847110

Dingerson, L. (1991). Reclaiming the gavel: Making sense out of the death penalty debate in state legislatures. *N.Y.U. Review of Law & Social Change, 18*(3), 873–885. Retrieved from https://socialchangenyu.com/review/reclaiming-the-gavel-making-sense-out-of-the-death-penalty-debate-in-state-legislatures

Death Penalty Information Center. (2019a). The death penalty in 2019: Year end report. Retrieved from https://deathpenaltyinfo.org/facts-and-research/dpic-reports/dpic-year-end-reports/the-death-penalty-in-2019-year-end-report

Death Penalty Information Center. (2019b). Death sentences in the United States since 1977. Retrieved from https://deathpenaltyinfo.org/facts-and-research/sentencing-data/death-sentences-in-the-united-states-from-1977-by-state-and-by-year

Death Penalty Information Center. (2019c). Execution database. Retrieved from https://deathpenalty-info.org/executions/execution-database

Death Penalty Information Center. (2019d). Murder rates by state. Retrieved from https://deathpenaltyinfo.org/facts-and-research/murder-rates/murder-rates-by-state

Death Penalty Information Center. (2020). Legislative roundup. Retrieved from https://deathpenaltyinfo.org/stories/legislative-roundup-recent-legislative-activity-as-of-march-7

Entzeroth, L. S. (2012). The end of the beginning: The politics of death and the American death penalty regime in the twenty-first century. *Oregon Law Review, 90*(3), 797–836. Retrieved from http://hdl.handle.net/1794/12127

Fenno, R. F. (1973). *Congressmen in committees.* Boston, MA: Little, Brown and Co.

Galliher, J. M., & Galliher, J. F. (1997). 'Déjà vu all over again': The recurring life and death of capital punishment legislation in Kansas. *Social Problems, 44,* 369–385. doi:10.2307/3097183

Galliher, J. F., Ray, G., & Cook, B. (1992). Abolition and reinstatement of capital punishment during the Progressive Era and early 20th century. *The Journal of Criminal Law and Criminology, 83*(3), 538–576. Retrieved from https://scholarlycommons.law.northwestern.edu/jclc/vol83/iss3/3

Galliher, J. F., Koch, L. W., Keys, D. P., & Guess, T. J. (2002). *America without the death penalty: States leading the way.* Boston, MA: Northeastern University Press.

Garland, D. (2010). *Peculiar institution: America's death penalty in an age of abolition.* Cambridge, MA: The Belkap Press of Harvard University Press.

Gerber, E. R. (1999). *The populist paradox: Interest group influence and the promise of direct legislation.* Princeton, NJ: Princeton University Press.

Hall, R. L. (1996). *Participation in Congress.* New Haven, CT: Yale University Press.

Harcourt, B. E. (2008). *Abolition in the U.S.A. by 2050: On political capital and ordinary acts of resistance.* John M. Olin Program in Law and Economics Working Paper No. 434. Retrieved from https://ssrn.com/abstract=1278080

Henry, J. S. (2008). New Jersey's road to abolition. *Justice System Journal, 29*(3), 408–422. doi:10.1080/0098261X.2008.10767904

Hilbe, J. M. (2011). *Negative binomial regression* (2nd ed.). New York, NY: Cambridge University Press.

Holian, D. B. (2004). He's stealing my issues! Clinton's crime rhetoric and the dynamics of issue ownership. *Political Behavior, 26*(2), 95–124. doi:10.1023/B:POBE.0000035959.35567.16

Holman, M. R., & Mahoney, A. M. (2019). The choice is yours: Caucus typologies and collaboration in U.S. state legislatures. *Representation, 55*(1), 47–63. doi:10.1080/00344893.2019.1581079

Hood, R., & Hoyle, C. (Eds.). (2015). *The death penalty: A worldwide perspective* (5th ed.). Oxford: Oxford University Press.

Jacobs, D., & Carmichael, J. (2002). The political sociology of the death penalty: A pooled time-series analysis. *American Sociological Review, 67*(1), 109–131. doi:10.2307/3088936

Jones, B. (2018). The Republican Party, conservatives, and the future of capital punishment. *The Journal of Criminal Law & Criminology, 108*(2), 223–252. Retrieved from https://ssrn.com/abstract=3002188

Jones, J. (2019). Americans now support life in prison over death penalty. *Gallup News Service.* Retrieved from https://news.gallup.com/poll/268514/americans-support-life-prison-death-penalty.aspx

Kaplan, A. (2013). Oregon's death penalty: The practical reality. *Lewis & Clark Law Review, 17*(1), 1–68. Retrieved from https://ssrn.com/abstract=2141502

Karch, A. (2007). *Democratic laboratories: Policy diffusion among the American states.* Ann Arbor, MI: University of Michigan Press.

Kirchmeier, J. L. (2006). Casting a wider net: Another decade of legislative expansion of the death penalty in the United States. *Pepperdine Law Review, 34*(1), 1–39. Retrieved from https://ssrn.com/abstract=959400

Kent, S. L. (2010). Predicting abolition: A cross-national survival analysis of the social and political determinants of death penalty statutes. *International Criminal Justice Review, 20*(1), 56–72. doi:10.1177/1057567709360333

Klarner, C. (2013). *State partisan balance data, 1937–2011.* Harvard Dataverse, V1. Retrieved from https://doi.org/10.7910/DVN/LZHMG3

Koch, L. W., & Galliher, J. F. (1993). Michigan's continuing abolition of the death penalty and the conceptual components of symbolic legislation. *Social and Legal Studies, 2*(3), 323–346. doi:10.1177/096466399300200304

Kousser, T. (2005). *Term limits and the dismantling of state legislative professionalism.* New York, NY: Cambridge University Press.

La Corte, R., & Johnson, G. (2018, October 12). Washington state ends 'racially biased' death penalty. *Associated Press.* Retrieved from https://apnews.com/e06f6693bfb645da95053e22fae8fd83

Langer, L., & Brace, P. (2005). The preemptive power of state supreme courts: Adoption of abortion and death penalty legislation. *Policy Studies Journal, 33*(3), 317–340. doi:10.1111/j.1541-0072.2005.00118.x

Lax, J. R., & Phillips, J. H. (2009). Gay rights in the states: Public opinion and policy responsiveness. *American Political Science Review, 103*(3), 367–386. doi:10.1017/S0003055409990050

Long, J. S. (1997). *Regression models for categorical and limited dependent variables.* Thousand Oaks, CA: Sage Publications.

Martin, R. J. (2010). Killing capital punishment in New Jersey: The first state in modern history to repeal its death penalty statute. *University of Toledo Law Review, 41*, 485–543. Retrieved from https://works.bepress.com/robert_martin/1

Masci, D. (2017). *5 Facts about the death penalty.* Pew Research Center. Retrieved from http://www.pewresearch.org/fact-tank/2017/04/24/5-facts-about-the-death-penalty

McCann, M., & Johnson, D. T. (2009). Rocked but still rolling: The enduring institution of capital punishment in historical and comparative perspective. In C. J. Ogletree, Jr & A. Sarat (Eds.), *Road to abolition? The future of capital punishment in the United States* (pp. 139–180). New York, NY: New York University Press.

Milleman, M. (2010). Limiting death: Maryland's new death penalty law. *Maryland Law Review, 70*(1), 272–306. Retrieved from https://digitalcommons.law.umaryland.edu/mlr/vol70/iss1/10

National Conference on State Legislatures. (2011). Annual vs. biennial legislative sessions. Retrieved from https://www.ncsl.org/research/about-state-legislatures/annual-vs-biennial-legislative-sessions.aspx

National Conference on State Legislatures. (2015). The term-limited states. Retrieved from https://www.ncsl.org/research/about-state-legislatures/chart-of-term-limits-states.aspx

National Conference on State Legislatures. (2020). State partisan composition. Retrieved from https://www.ncsl.org/research/about-state-legislatures/partisan-composition.aspx

Nice, D. C. (1992). The states and the death penalty. *Western Political Quarterly, 45*(4), 1037–1048. doi:10.2307/448824

Parker, N. M. (2013). The road to abolition: How widespread legislative repeal of the death penalty in the states could catalyze a nationwide ban on capital punishment. *Legislation and Policy Brief, 5*(1), 65–102. Retrieved from https://digitalcommons.wcl.american.edu/lpb/vol5/iss1/3/

Radelet, M. (2017). *The history of the death penalty in Colorado.* Boulder, CO: University Press of Colorado.

Radelet, M., & Lacock, T. L. (2009). Do executions lower homicide rates?: The views of leading criminologists. *Journal of Criminal Law and Criminology, 99*(2), 489–508. Retrieved from https://scholarlycommons.law.northwestern.edu/jclc/vol99/iss2/4

Ruddell, R., & Urbina, M. G. (2004). Minority threat and punishment: A cross-national analysis. *Justice Quarterly, 21*(4), 903–931. doi:10.1080/07418820400096031

Sarat, A. (2001). *When the state kills.* Princeton, NJ: Princeton University Press.

Sarat, A. (2002). The 'new abolitionism' and the possibilities of legislative action: The New Hampshire experience. *Ohio State Law Journal, 63*(1), 343–369. Retrieved from http://hdl.handle.net/1811/70489

Sarat, A., Malague, J., De los Santos, L., Pedersen, K., Qasim, N., Seymour, L., & Wishloff, S. (2019). When the death penalty goes public: Referendum, initiative, and the fate of capital punishment. *Law & Social Inquiry, 44*(2), 391–419. doi:10.1111/lsi.12360

Schiller, W. J. (1995). Senators as political entrepreneurs: Using bill sponsorship to shape legislative agendas. *American Journal of Political Science, 39*(1), 186–203. doi:10.2307/2111763

Soss, J., Langbein, L., & Metelko, A. R. (2003). Why do white Americans support the death penalty? *The Journal of Politics, 65*(2), 397–421. doi:10.1111/1468-2508.t01-2-00006

Steiker, C. S. (2002). Capital punishment and American exceptionalism. *Oregon Law Review, 81*(1), 97–130. Retrieved from http://hdl.handle.net/1794/4366

Steiker, C. S. (2012). Review: Capital punishment and contingency. *Harvard Law Review, 125*(3), 760–787. Retrieved from https://harvardlawreview.org/2012/01/capital-punishment-and-contingency

Steiker, C. S., & Steiker, J. M. (2006). A tale of two nations: Implementation of the death penalty in "executing" versus "symbolic" states in the United States. *Texas Law Review, 84*(7), 1869–1927.

Steiker, C. S., & Steiker, J. M. (2014). The death penalty and mass incarceration: Convergences and divergences. *American Journal of Criminal Law, 41*(2), 189–207.

Squire, P. (1992). Legislative professionalization and membership diversity in state legislatures. *Legislative Studies Quarterly, 17*(1), 69–79.

Squire, P. (1998). Membership turnover and the efficient processing of legislation. *Legislative Studies Quarterly, 23*(1), 23–32. doi:10.2307/440212

Squire, P. (2007). Measuring legislative professionalism: The Squire index revisited. *State Politics & Policy Quarterly, 7*(2), 211–227. doi:10.1177/153244000700700208

Squire, P. (2012). *The evolution of American legislatures: Colonies, territories, and states, 1619–2009.* Ann Arbor, MI: University of Michigan Press.

Squire, P. (2017). A Squire index update. *State Politics & Policy Quarterly, 17*(4), 1–11. doi:10.1177/1532440017713314

Squire, P., & Moncrief, G. (2019). *State legislatures today: Politics under the domes* (3rd ed.). Lanham, MD: Rowman & Littlefield.

Vidmar, N., & Ellsworth, E. (1974). Public opinion and the death penalty. *Stanford Law Review, 26*, 1245–1270. Retrieved from https://scholarship.law.duke.edu/faculty_scholarship/519

Warden, R. (2012). How and why Illinois abolished the death penalty. *Law & Inequality, 30*(2), 245–286. Retrieved from http://scholarship.law.umn.edu/lawineq/vol30/iss2/2

Wasserman, M. (2018, March 8). Efforts to ban the death penalty fizzle out in Legislature. *The News Tribune.* Retrieved from https://www.thenewstribune.com/news/politics-government/article204222859.html

Wawro, G. (2000). *Legislative entrepreneurship in the U.S. House of Representatives.* Ann Arbor, MI: University of Michigan Press.

Williams, K. (2012). *Most deserving of death?: An analysis of the Supreme Court's death penalty jurisprudence.* Farnham: Ashgate.

Wright, G. C., & Schaffner, B. F. (2002). The influence of party: Evidence from the state legislatures. *American Political Science Review, 96*(2), 367–379. doi:10.1017/S0003055402000229

Wozniak, K. H. (2012). Legislative abolition of the death penalty: A qualitative analysis. *Studies in Law, Politics, and Society, 57*, 31–70. doi:10.1108/S1059-4337(2012)0000057005

Zimring, F. E. & Hawkins, G. (1986). *Capital punishment and the American agenda.* New York, NY: Cambridge University Press.

CASES CITED

Atkins v. *Virginia*, 536 US 304 (2002).

Furman v. *Georgia*, 408 US 238 (1972).

Kennedy v. *Louisiana*, 554 US 407 (2008).

Ring v. *Arizona*, 536 US 584 (2002).

Roper v. *Simmons*, 543 US 551 (2005).

APPENDIX 1: CODING OF THE DEPENDENT VARIABLE

To construct the two main categories of bills – *restrictive* and *supportive* – all bills were initially coded based upon a number of subcategories:

Restrictive Bills	Supportive Bills
(1a) Repeals the death penalty or creates a moratorium	(2a) Disfavors the defendant in the pre-trial, trial, appeals- or execution process
(1b) Favors the defendant in the pre-trial, trial, appeals- or execution process	(2b) Expands the death penalty, for example, adds a death penalty-eligible crime
(1c) Narrows the death penalty, for example, removes a death penalty-eligible crime	
(1d) Creates a study or commission	

Some bills combine two or more subcategories; a common combination is a bill that intends to both create a moratorium and a commission to study the death penalty. Such bills are, however, only counted once, and in such cases as moratorium bills. In rare cases, comprehensive criminal justice reform bills amend the law in ways that both favor and disfavor a capital defendant. One such bill is included in this study (HB663, enacted in OH in 2014), and has been split to count as two separate bills. The collection of bills includes 151 resolutions (about 4.5% of the total). While resolutions are not as likely to have policy content and do not typically have the effect of a law, without them important data would be lost, such as about one third of all bills urging for various types of state studies of the use of capital punishment.

APPENDIX 2: SUMMARY STATISTICS

	M	SD	Min	Max	*N*
Restrictive bill introductions	2.90	4.61	0	45	709
Supportive bill introductions	1.90	2.61	0	17	709
Active legislator(s) restrictive bills	0.15	0.30	0	1	709
Active legislator(s) supportive bills	0.07	0.22	0	1	709
Bipartisanship restrictive bills	0.24	0.36	0	1	709
Bipartisanship supportive bills	0.20	0.35	0	1	709
Republican house	0.58	0.49	0	1	709
Republican senate	0.65	0.48	0	1	709
Republican governor	0.58	0.49	0	1	709
Legislative professionalism	0.19	0.12	0.03	0.63	709
Term limits	0.33	0.47	0	1	709
Death sentences	3.00	5.47	0	48	709
Executions	1.39	3.94	0	40	709
State homicide rate	5.10	2.32	0.83	14.20	709
Biennial session	0.18	0.32	0	1	709
Total no. of bills (100s)	22.10	23.93	0	205.11	709

APPENDIX 3: CODING OF INDEPENDENT VARIABLES AND SOURCES OF DATA

Variable	Measurement	Source
Active legislator(s) restrictive/ supportive bills	A combination of two measurements (author's own calculation): Percentage of the total annual number of bills introduced by one lawmaker or cohesive group of lawmakers: 1. In 1 year representing a disproportional amount of the total number of bills, but corresponding to at least three 2. Over a period of at least 3 years representing at least one bill each year	Data on sponsors of bills from websites of state legislatures
Bipartisanship restrictive/ supportive bills	Percentage of total annual number of bills with bipartisan sponsorship (author's own calculation). Bipartisan defined as at least 20% of bill sponsors belonging to the opposite party	Data on sponsors of bills from websites of state legislatures
Republican house	House controlled by the Republican Party (1/0)	Klarner (2013) for years 1999–2011. National Conference of State Legislatures (2020) for years 2012–2018
Republican senate	Senate controlled by the Republican Party (1/0)	Klarner (2013) for years 1999–2011. National Conference of State Legislatures (2020) for years 2012–2018. For Nebraska, data on party affiliation for the state's senators obtained via Nebraska's Clerk of the Legislature's Blue Book archive (various years)
Republican governor	Governor is Republican (1/0)	Klarner (2013) for years 1999–2011. National Conference of State Legislatures (2020) for years 2012–2018
Legislative professionalism	The Squire index is available for years 1996, 2003, 2009 and 2015. Values for missing years imputed via Stata	Squire (2012, 2017)
Term limits	Dummy variable indicating states have term limits for legislators (1/0)	National Conference of State Legislatures (2015)
Death sentences	Annual number of death sentences	Death Penalty Information Center (2019b)
Executions	Annual number of executions	Death Penalty Information Center (2019c)
State homicide rate	Annual state homicide rate	Death Penalty Information Center (2019d)
Biennial session	Dummy variable indicating states have biennial sessions (1/0)	National Conference on State Legislatures (2011)
Total no. of bills (100s)	The total number of bills introduced each year, divided by 100	Council of State Governments (various years)

SECTION II

HATRED AND THE LAW:
A SYMPOSIUM

CHAPTER 2

LACK OF PUNISHMENT DOESN'T FIT THE CRIME: AMERICA'S TEPID RESPONSE TO BIAS-MOTIVATED CRIME

Jeannine Bell

ABSTRACT

For more than a decade, public opinion polls have shown that nearly 80% of Americans support hate crime legislation as a response to violence committed because of the victim's race, color, religion, and sexual orientation. Americans' widespread support for legislation aimed at bias-motivated crimes is not matched by the federal and state efforts devoted to responding to such crimes. This chapter describes the myriad factors contributing to America's limited police and prosecutorial response to hate crimes. After a discussion of the patchwork of state and federal legislation aimed at hate crimes, the chapter analyzes the substantial legislative and administrative structures that hamper the enforcement of hate crime law in the United States.

Keywords: Hate crime; policing; criminal justice; race; bias crime; legislation

INTRODUCTION

On March 19, 2019, during Friday prayer in Christchurch, New Zealand, a gunman went to two mosques and began shooting at the gathered worshipers. Forty-nine people were killed; scores were injured. A manifesto the suspect posted on line

Studies in Law, Politics, and Society, Volume 85, 29–48
Copyright © 2021 by Emerald Publishing Limited
All rights of reproduction in any form reserved
ISSN: 1059-4337/doi:10.1108/S1059-433720210000085003

spoke of the white nationalist aims of the shooting. Although it was the deadliest, the shooting in Christchurch echoed two other hate murders at places of worship in the United States – a massacre at Pittsburgh synagogue in October 2018 by a white supremacist, which killed 11 people, and the shootings at a black church in Charleston in 2017, also by a white supremacist which killed nine worshipers.

Horrifying hate murders are just one segment of what is happening with hate crime – crimes motivated by bias on the basis of race, religion, sexual orientation, gender, and other categories – in America. In 2017, the FBI, which aggregates data submitted by law enforcement agencies, reported 7,175 individual bias incidents occurred that year in America. Responding to these more than 7,175+ incidents presents the greatest law enforcement problem of hate crime in America (FBI, 2018). These incidents may be less sensational but they are constant, multiple, and systemic.

In fact, the scope of the problem is likely even larger than the FBI numbers suggest. For a variety of reasons that I will discuss later in this chapter, the FBI statistics undercount the number of hate crimes. The only other government source of data on hate crime, the National Crime Victimization Survey (NCVS), reports a larger number. The NCVS, described in more detail later, is a national survey of households which collects data using the same definition of hate crimes as the FBI.[1] In 2017, the National Crime Victimization survey estimated, based on their survey results, that each year between 2013 and 2017 Americans reported experiencing approximately 200,000 hate crimes (Department of Justice). Further, experts connected with this survey believe that fewer than 50%, just 101,900 hate crimes were reported to the police, which reflects a significant difference with police numbers for those years (Department of Justice). Obviously, police and state and federal prosecutors are central to any state response to hate crime. For example, if police do not recognize appropriate incidents as hate crimes, hate crime law is likely to be under enforced. Similarly, if prosecutors fail to bring hate crime charges, in most cases, hate crime laws cannot be utilized.

After a description of the legal landscape for bias-motivated crime, this chapter explores how the law in this area functions in actuality. Part II of the chapter engages with the shortcomings of this legal landscape despite more than 30 years of targeted responses to bias-motivated crime. In the final section of the chapter, I question whether the problems documented, in fact, stem from Americans' inability to empathize or support victims who are targeted by hate crime. That is, is this another instance of how systemic racism in American society shows itself?

PART I. THE LEGISLATIVE RESPONSE: THE CREATION OF HATE CRIMES LAW

Acts of bias-motivated crime have a long-standing history in the United States committed by organized groups like the Ku Klux Klan dedicated to terrorizing Blacks and other marginalized groups. But, it was not until the 1980s that the term, "hate crime," began to be used by advocates who started to track the numbers of hate crimes committed (Wolfe, 2018). Thus, hate crime law is a fairly recent invention. Before 1980, the state of Connecticut alone had legislation aimed at criminalizing acts of bias motivation. It took until the mid-90s for the enactment of federal legislation providing additional penalties for bias-motivated crime.

Scholars trace the origin of hate crime laws to social movement activity (Jenness & Grattet, 2001). The gay and lesbian, women's and civil rights movements created a space for a discussion of the rights of hate crime victims (Jenness & Grattet, 2001). Once this had happened, the hate crime victim movement began to document instances of violence and, then, to campaign for a way to address this violence. Interestingly, some scholars characterize this creation of hate crime law as an exercise of symbolic politics, rather than a legislative response sincerely targeting constituent needs and demands (Haider-Markel, 1998; Jacobs & Potter, 1998).

State Responses to Hate Crimes

Many advocates seeking a remedy on behalf of hate crime victims targeted state legislatures. The majority of hate crimes, like most criminal law, are prosecuted at the state level. Advocates urged passage of modern hate crime laws, following in the wake of 1960s era anti-mask[2] and institutional vandalism statutes.[3] Over the course of the 1980s, 1990s, and in 2000s, often in the response to lobbying, most states passed hate crime laws. As of March 2019, all but 5 states had hate crime legislation (Wolfe, 2018).

The most common type of state hate crime law is a penalty enhancement statute. Penalty enhancement statutes allow perpetrators to receive greater penalties if the prosecutor can demonstrate beyond a reasonable doubt that the offender deliberately selected the victim because of one of the proscribed characteristics, based on the perpetrator's bias against the victim (Lieberman & Freeman, 2009). Many state statutes reflect the basic structure of the model hate crime statute created by the Anti-Defamation League (ADL) in 1981. Because many state statutes are designed around the model statute, the vast majority punish attacks motivated by bias on the basis of race, religion, and national origin/ethnicity. This is where their similarity and uniformity end. Overall, there is a patchwork of offense structures; only 31 states have penalty enhancement statutes specially punishing crimes motivated by bias on the basis of sexual orientation; 30 states include disability in the list of characteristics perpetrators may run afoul of in hate crime law; and 26 states proscribe crimes committed because of the victim's gender (Lieberman & Freeman, 2009). Other categories referenced by a small number of states include gender identity and political affiliation (Washington, DC; Iowa) (Wolfe, 2018). Thus, across the states with these laws, there is considerable variety in what types of bias are recognized as constituent of hate crimes.

Federal Legislative Responses

Most hate crimes are punished under the state law, but federal law has an important role in cases where states are unwilling or unable to prosecute crimes. The first use of the term "hate crime" in federal legislation was in the Hate Crimes Statistics Act (HCSA) of 1990. The HCSA required the US Attorney General to collect data on crimes, "that evidenced prejudice based on race, religion, sexual orientation, or ethnicity" (Hate Crime Statistics Act). Disability was added to this list of characteristics in 1994. Ultimately, the director of the FBI turned the job of collecting and managing hate crime data to the Uniform Crime Reporting (UCR) Program. The UCR requests numbers from all state, federal, and local law enforcement agencies in a variety of areas including hate crime. The FBI also provided guidance to police departments which were unfamiliar with the hate crime category. The FBI developed and promulgated hate crime data collection guidelines to assist police departments (Wolfe, 2018).

The HCSA is only a data collection statute; it records but does not punish hate crimes. It was not until 4 years later, in 1994, when the Violent Crime Control and Law Enforcement Act mandated that the US Sentencing Commission create guidelines for hate crime penalty enhancement for existing offenses under federal law. The resulting US Sentencing Guidelines section 3A 1.1 (a) were to provide the following adjustments in sentences for any federal offenses in these circumstances:

> if the finder of fact at trial or in the case of a plea of guilty or nolo contendere, the court in sentencing determines beyond a reasonable doubt that the defendant intentionally selected any victim or any property as the object of the offense of conviction because of the actual or perceived race, color, religion, national origin, ethnicity, gender, disability, or sexual orientation of any person, increase by three levels. (US sentencing guidelines section 3A 1.1a)

This hate crime sentencing enhancement statute creates space for the punishment of bias-motivated behavior in a wide variety of circumstances; previous legislation had only allowed hate crimes to be prosecuted under 1960s era legislation prohibiting interference with civil rights.

The federal response to hate crime continued to expand throughout the 1990s. The pinnacle of activist lobbying for hate crime legislation occurred in 1998 when President George Bush signed the Matthew Shepard James Byrd Hate Crime Prevention Act (HCPA). The HCPA provides financial resources to states and tribes to help investigate and prosecute hate crimes. In addition, it creates a new federal crime in situations in which an individual uses fire or a dangerous weapon to willfully cause injury to another individual. The Act applies when:

1. the crime was committed because of the actual or perceived race, color, religion, national origin of any person or:
2. the crime was committed because of the actual or perceived religion, national origin, gender, sexual orientation, gender identity, or disability of any person and the crime affected interstate or foreign commerce or occurred within federal special maritime and territorial jurisdiction.

Before the passage of these pieces of federal legislation, hate crimes could be punished only under federal civil rights law, Title 18, U.S.C §241, and §242, which required the defendant to have interfered with the victim's participation in an activity that the government acknowledged as protected by federal civil rights. The HCPA is broader than this previous legislation as it does not require the government prove anything other than bias motivation.

The James Byrd Matthew Shepard Act was the first piece of federal legislation specifically directed at criminalizing bias-motivated crime in situations where local prosecution of hate crime was not available. As such not only was it a fitting tribute to the victims of these two horrific hate murders, but also spoke to the issue of state failure regarding hate crime. The Act was named for two high profile victims of hate crime, Matthew Shepard, a gay college student, was killed in Wyoming and James Byrd, a Black man who was dragged behind a truck in Texas until he died. Both men were killed in states that did not have hate crime legislation at the time of their murders.

PART II. TESTING THE ADEQUACY OF THE STATE'S RESPONSE

The passage of laws, and the stipulation of collection of data on hate crime, have little impact if perpetrators are rarely charged under the laws or if law enforcement never collects data regarding hate crime. This section evaluates the strength of states' responses by looking first to one of the most critical levers in any response to hate crime – the police. After all, police are responsible for responding to hate incidents, investigating hate crimes, and forwarding case files to prosecutors for hate crime charges. Police officers are a critical factor in state response; as the first stage in the criminal justice process, if the police decide to dismiss the report of a hate crime, it most likely will never receive any other attention (Bell, 2002). Additionally, police officers have early contact with victims of hate crime, and the police treatment of hate crime victim's cases can have an important impact on victim's experience. Finally, as those responsible for filing reports to the FBI, under the HCSA, the police have the opportunity to provide one of the most comprehensive national picture of hate crime in the United States.

Data Collection

One of the earliest national measures of hate crime was the HCSA. The FBI collected reports from law enforcement agencies around the country. Thus, one way of evaluating the reach of law enforcement of hate crime as a serious problem is to track FBI numbers. Increasingly high numbers of hate crime could signal that more hate crimes are being committed in a particular area. For this to be a credible explanation, one might expect triggering events – for instance, in the wake of the 9/11 attacks, hate crimes directed at Muslims increased in several different jurisdictions around the country (FBI, 2011). In the absence of any particular event, policy changes in hate crime classification or identification may result in law enforcement officers simply getting better at identifying and classifying hate crime, and, thus, results in increased numbers recorded.

FBI Hate Crime Statistics, 1992–2007

The FBI data collected under the HCSA are the only government data presenting a national picture, individualized by state and locality of hate crime. The results from the first 15 years of this data collection, from 1992 to 2007, show wide variation in how law enforcement agencies approach the task of collecting and submitting data on hate crime (Lieberman & Freeman, 2009). The second FBI report of hate crime in 1993 indicated that 7,466 hate crimes occurred in 1992 and was based on data collected by 61,811 agencies in 42 states including the District of Columbia (Lieberman & Freeman, 2009). These agencies covered just 51% of the US population. By 2007, the number of states with law enforcement agencies submitting a hate crime report to the FBI had risen to 50 (including the District of Columbia). The number of agencies reporting more than doubled from the 1991 figures, increasing to 13,241. This huge increase in the number of reporting agencies meant that more of the US population was represented in the report. Police agencies serving, collectively, 85% of the population reported the number of hate crimes in their jurisdictions by 2007 (Lieberman & Freeman, 2009).

Despite significant increases in the number of reporting agencies, the FBI data on hate crime show very little increase in the number of hate crimes reported. With the exception of 2001, the year of the 9/11 attacks, the number of hate crimes reported by law enforcement agencies largely remains flat (see Table 1). Zeroing in on the data reported by individual law enforcement agencies shows that despite more agencies reporting, a large percentage of agencies reported that not a single hate crime occurred in their jurisdiction. For instance, in 2007, of the 13,241 law enforcement agencies – police departments and sheriffs agencies – reporting hate crimes in 2007, the vast majority, 11,284, or 84% of the total number of agencies, reported *no* hate crimes in the previous year. In other words, the data from the hate crime 2007 report came from just 2,025 agencies reporting that that one or more hate crime had occurred in their jurisdiction. The submission of data to the FBI by individual agencies is voluntary, in the majority of states. Only 27 states and the District of Columbia require law enforcement agencies to report hate crime. Given the lack of strict reporting requirements, more than 4,000 law enforcement did not participate at all in the FBI reporting. This suggests that in these agencies, hate crime laws not being enforced.

FBI Hate Crime Statistics, 2008–2017

Low numbers of hate crimes in the first years of FBI reporting are unsurprising. One might assume that it would take some time for agencies to adopt hate crime polices and then begin to effectively use the FBI guidelines. Unfortunately, FBI statistics offers little evidence that law enforcement agencies improved in their ability to track hate crime between 2008 and 2017. The FBI hate crime statistics from 2008 to 2017 (see Table 2) are nearly flat, showing relatively little increase in the number of hate crimes reported, over the earliest years of reporting. This is even more troubling given that the number of agencies reporting hate crime increased. Despite thousands of more agencies reporting, the overall numbers of hate crimes did not increase. How do we account for this?

So long as there are no indications to the contrary, a lack of an increase in the number of hate crimes with more agencies reporting would not necessarily suggest that hate crime law is not being fully enforced. Other analyses suggest that the FBI data missed hate crimes that occurred. There are two main elements to the assertion that FBI data – which stems from police reports – are inadequate.

Table 1. Hate Crime Statistics, 1996–2007.

	1996	1997	1998	1999	2000	2001	2002	2003	2004	2005	2006	2007
Participating agencies	11,354	11,211	10,730	12,122	11,690	11,987	12,073	11,909	12,711	12,417	12,620	13,241
Total hate crime incidents reported	8,759	8,049	7,755	7,876	8,063	9,730	7,462	7,489	7,649	7,163	7,722	7,624
Percentage of US population agencies represented (%)	82.82	81.66	78.31	83.36	83.97	84.85	85.96	83.04	86.81	82.91	85.49	86.39
Number of agencies that reported 0 hate crimes	9,520	9,479	8,920	10,307	9,798	9,881	10,205	9,942	10,665	10,380	10,515	11,216
Percentage of agencies reporting 0 hate crimes (%)	83.85	84.55	83.13	85.03	83.82	82.43	84.53	83.48	83.90	83.60	83.32	84.71

Source: https://ucr.fbi.gov/hate-crime/.

Table 2. Hate Crime Statistics, 2008–2017.

	2008	2009	2010	2011	2012	2013	2014	2015	2016	2017
Participating agencies	13,690	14,422	14,977	14,575	13,022	15,016	15,494	14,997	15,254	16,149
Total hate crime incidents reported	7,783	6,604	6,628	6,222	5,796	5,928	5,479	5,850	6,121	7,175
Percentage of US population agencies represented (%)	88.59	90.93	92.13	91.77	79.24	93.29	93.50	88.43	89.61	94.08
Number of agencies that reported 0 hate crimes	11,545	12,388	13,028	12,631	11,292	13,190	13,828	13,255	13,478	14,109
Percentage of agencies reporting 0 hate crimes (%)	84.33	85.90	86.99	86.71	86.71	87.84	89.25	88.38	88.36	87.37

Source: https://ucr.fbi.gov/hate-crime.

The first claim is that FBI data fail to capture hates crimes because those targeted by hate crime do not report these crimes. Research into the failure of victims to report hate crimes to the police by Pezzella, Fetzer, and Keller compared the large gap between the 2004 and 2012 NCVS estimate of hate crimes committed and the FBI reports of the same time period. Looking to whether these police face difficulty getting reports of crimes involving bias crime, the authors found that victims of bias crime victims are less likely to report an attack than victims of non-bias motivated crime (Pezzella et al., 2019). According to this research, many hate crime victims decide not to report because they do not see police officers as legitimate and do not think that police will help (Pezzella et al., 2019).

Underreporting can certainly affect the accuracy of FBI data. But, another criticism has suggested that the data are wrong in ways that are more attributable to a failure to collect and then to report accurately. In other words, there are hate crimes police departments know about that are not included in the FBI reports. Advocacy organizations, scholarly centers, and news organizations collecting data on hate crime suggest that police departments may fail to report hate crimes to the FBI even when the bias motive is acknowledged by police. For instance, the Center for the Study of Hate and Extremism notes that the 2016 Pulse nightclub massacre in Orlando, widely recognized as an anti-gay hate crime, was not included in FBI figures (Center for the Study of Hate & Extremism, 2017). Another investigative report by BuzzFeed news examined more than 2,400 police incident reports from 10 of the largest police departments reporting no hate crimes to the FBI in 2016. In reading the reports, analysts identified 15 assaults in which the investigating officers' written narratives suggested bias motivation. Independent experts reviewed the documents and agreed that each of the 15 cases should have been flagged as possible hate crimes and investigated (Aldhous, 2018).

With so much data missing from the FBI figures on hate crime, it is very hard to establish a baseline number of hate crime committed, and thus, whether such crimes have been increasing over time. One of the most significant differences in the number of hate crimes reported by the FBI from the estimates offered by NCVS survey is the number of hate crimes that victims say are reported to the police. The NCVS survey shows significant differences with FBI data, even when we take into account the differences in the sources (official statistics vs lay reports). Criminologists expect differences between victim-reported data and police data. A third criteria, perhaps the most reliable,[4] included situations where the victim reported that the police investigation confirmed that a hate crime occurred. Between 2013 and 2017, on an average, the NCVS reported that of the 101,000 hate crimes reported to the police, in 15,200 victims noted that the police agreed that the incident was a hate crime. This figure is twice as large as the number reported by the UCR.

Explaining Police Officers' Failure to "Recognize" Hate Crimes

Though the HCSA provides an aggregate nationwide picture of hate crime, there are many downsides to this particular form of federal data collection. First, at this point, the HCSA does not capture all hate crimes. The HCSA collects only hate crimes reflecting the categories of race, religion, disability, ethnic/national origin, and sexual orientation. State and localities hate crime statutes may vary in the categories covered, and the offense punished (Nolan et al., 2015). Moreover, states may have categories like gender identity included in their hate crime laws that are not covered by the HCSA. The latter group of crimes would have to be removed and not submitted to the FBI. In addition to the difficulty created by removing crimes, research has shown that police officers viewed the phrase "motivated in whole or in part by bias" in the FBI's guidelines to be ambiguous (Nolan & Akyama, 2002). In addition to frustrating officers, the mismatch between state and federal hate crime statutes and confusion created with the wording of bias-motivation may be part of reason the FBI report does not accurately capture the real number of hate crimes.

Several examinations of police officers' approach to investigating hate crime have found that police struggle so much that they may be failing to identify hate crimes (Bell, 2009; Garafalo, 1991; Glickhouse, 2019; Johnson, 2018; Martin, 1995). In some cases, this may stem from a lack of policies focused on hate crime. Studies of several different police agencies found that even in states with robust hate crime law approximately 40% of police agencies did not have written hate crime policies (Johnson, 2019). Other studies suggest that even when departments have a policy in place and officers are specifically charged with investigating hate crime, they may develop a heighted standard for what constitutes bias, only classifying as hate crimes those with the most extreme signs of bias (Boyd, Berk, & Hamner, 1996; McDevitt, Levin, & Bennett, 2002; Nolan et al., 2015). Though exactly how many hate crimes are weeded out as a result of police processes is not known, one study that examined hate crimes in New Jersey revealed that investigators referred just 5% of the cases that were given as potential hate crimes to prosecutors for investigation (Phillips, 2009).

Most critically, officers' difficulty identifying hate crime may stem from their lack of support for hate crime laws. Research by Boyd et al. (1996) evaluated how officers in two divisions of a police department struggled with hate crime classification. Police were dismissive of hate crimes, calling them, "overkill," "mostly bull," "a pain in the ass," "media hype" (Boyd et al., 1996, p. 827). One division underenforced hate crime law and the other over enforced it; neither division adopted strategies which were demonstrated careful attention to bias-crime law. A study of police bias units from Maryland and New York City found officers struggling to identify bias motivation in the face of secondary motivation. The officers also did not know what, if any, weight to give to conflicting stories told by the victim and perpetrators (Garafalo & Martin, 1993).

These studies in which police officers struggle with hate crime, or decline to investigate it, contrast sharply with one description of a well-organized and funded department containing officers who took seriously their charge to investigate hate crime. This unusual unit was "Center City's" Anti-Bias Task force, a 19-person, mixed race, and gender specialized detective unit charged with investigating hate crime (Bell, 2002). In contrast with the law enforcement officers described by Boyd, the officers in Center City were detectives responsible for following up initial reports. The specialized nature of their jobs was significant. As detectives who worked in a specialized unit which only investigated hate crime, they were repeat players in that area, seeing many cases of hate crime each year. This allowed them to develop critical routines for dealing with the vagaries of hate crime. These routines helped the detectives process many of the difficulties that other law enforcement officers experienced – distinguishing between crimes in which perpetrators' use slurs and epithets because they are angry from those in which biased speech constitutes evidence of bias motivation. In this way, the ABTF detectives were able to distill bias motivation and separate it from protected speech (Bell, 2002).

Differences in Hate Crime Reporting

Unfortunately, for victims of hate crime, there is significant under enforcement of these laws. More than 30 years after the passage of the Hate Crime Statistics Act, many law enforcement agencies have not risen to challenge of enforcing hate crime legislation. Research has noted that hate crime reporting has been higher in the Northeast and west, and has been scant in the Black Belt (King, 2007; McVeigh, Welch, & Bjarnason, 2003). In 2017, 87.4% of agencies reported that no hate crimes occurred in their jurisdictions (FBI, 2007). If law enforcement agencies are reporting no hate crimes occurred in their jurisdiction, then citizens who live in these jurisdictions are most likely not afforded any "protection" association with hate crime law. The patchwork in reporting of hate crime is unsurprising given studies of the ways in which hate crime law is enforcement suggest a wide variety of enforcement mechanisms (Bell, 2002; Boyd, et al., 1996; Garafalo & Martin, 1993). In a few jurisdictions, hate crime law is enforced with dedicated hate crime police detective units charged solely with the enforcement of the law (Bell, 2002). In others, responsibility is given to isolated detective units who struggle with identifying and classifying hate crime (Boyd et al., 1996).

Research regarding the roots of individual police department's failure to participate in hate crime reporting just after the passage of hate crime law suggest that there are several variables or factors which increase the likelihood of reporting (Nolan & Akyama, 2002). In their survey of "good reporting agencies" and "non-reporting" agencies, Nolan and Akyama discovered marked differences in different police agencies' desires to support those victimized by hate crime and in officers' beliefs regarding the seriousness of hate crime and importance of reporting (p. 100). Officers in agencies that had a high level of institutionalization around hate crime – hate crime policies, procedures preventing misclassification of a crime and more supervisors who supported hate crime investigation – were more likely to report than officers located in departments where officers were poorly trained (Nolan & Akyama, 2002).

Explaining the Failures of Police Enforcement

The failure to accurately report the number of hate crimes committed in a jurisdiction is unsurprising given: (1) the legal terrain which officers must navigate; (2) the number tasks with which law enforcement officers must grapple in hate crime investigation; and (3) the complexity of hate crime investigation. Combining three different factors makes the job of investigating hate crime exceedingly difficult for officers.

With respect to legal terrain, officers are forced to navigate two confusing and potentially contradictory Supreme Court cases, *R.A.V.* v. *St. Paul* (1992) and *Wisconsin* v. *Mitchell* (1993). *R.A.V.* v. *St. Paul* involved a white skinhead's challenge to the city of St. Paul's bias motivated crime ordinance, after he was charged with violating the hate crime statute for having burned a cross on a black family's lawn.[5] In *R.A.V.*, the Supreme Court struck down the St. Paul statute on First Amendment grounds because it condemned one particular viewpoint. For police officers, this decision has the effect of preventing them from criminalizing hate speech as they enforce hate crime legislation. In other words, the Court's decision makes clear that police may not arrest defendants just for using hate speech.

The very next year, in the wake of several state court decisions invalidating hate crime laws, the Court decided *Wisconsin* v. *Mitchell*. This case involved the selection and assault of a white victim, by a black defendant. In *Mitchell*, there was clear evidence that the defendant had selected the victim because of his race. The Supreme Court reversed the Wisconsin Supreme Court, which had relied on *R.A.V.* to strike down Wisconsin's hate crime penalty enhancement statute on First Amendment grounds. According to the US Supreme Court, the Wisconsin statute did not violate the First Amendment because the use of the defendant's speech as evidence of his motive was permissible under the First Amendment. Taken together, these two Supreme Court decisions allow law enforcement officers to enforce hate crime laws so long as they are only using speech as evidence of the defendant's motivation. To do otherwise – to use of slurs or epithets as a reason for arresting or charging individuals — violates *R.A.V.*, which still remains good law.

Hate crimes are difficult for police officers to enforce because of the myriad tasks with which detectives must grapple. As the paragraph above suggests, because of Supreme Court case law, detectives enforcing hate crime law must identify bias motivation in a way that is entirely separate from just relying on slurs and epithets. Researchers who study perpetrators have identified several different types of hate crimes all of which have different motivations (McDevitt et al., 2002). Though hate crimes are all motivated by bias there is not just one story of bias motivation. Analysis of hundreds of hate crimes reveals that within the umbrella of bias, there are several different categories offenders' of motivations including thrill, defensive, mission, and retaliatory motivation (McDevitt et al., 2002). In thrill hate crimes, the offender is motivated by the power; defensive offenders are protecting their resources from conditions that they find threatening; mission offenders hope to "cleanse the earth of evil," and retaliatory offenders are acting because they want to avenge an assault or perceive degradation of their group (McDevitt et al., 2002, p. 306).

The complications created by hate crime law's focus on bias motivation and differing offender motivations require detailed police investigation. One study showcasing this evaluated eight police departments in the Southern, Eastern, Midwestern, and Western areas of the United States analyzing the ways in which officers structured their time based on different types of arrangements for dealing with bias crime (Cronin et al., 2007). Some departments had two levels of screening for hate crimes, while others had a single screening mechanism in which patrol officers had to decide whether an incident was bias-motivated. Law enforcement officers who had the opportunity to send potentially bias motivated crimes to a well-trained experienced bias crime unit for further investigation were most inclusive of potentially bias-motivated crimes (Cronin et al., 2007). By contrast, officers who were forced to make the determination on patrol, informally, applied a much more restrictive assessment "based on their personal experience with prior incidents, thereby potentially suppressing the number of bias crimes that are accurately identified" (Cronin et al., 2007, p. 225). In other words, the presence of well-trained, specialized units in a police department increases the likelihood that more hate crimes will be recognized by the police.

Police departments may vary significantly in how they treat, and whether they investigate hate crimes at all. If the police department does not fully investigate hate crime, then the police statistics will not be a reliable account of the number of hate crimes that have occurred in the particular jurisdiction. If police departments do not have mechanisms for investigating hate crimes, then the department may report no hate crimes having occurred in their particular jurisdiction. Even if a department has a good approach to investigating and following up on hate crime, there are other ways that the numbers of hate crimes that are actually reported can be affected. Because hate crimes are viewed by most individuals as racist events, politicians may put pressures on the section of the department responsible for investigating hate crime to avoid having the city labeled as "racist" (Bell, 2002, 2013).

The Prosecution of Hate Crimes

About 88% of the agencies submitting reports to the FBI in 2017 reported that no hate crimes occurred in their jurisdiction. It is hard to classify the failure to report hate crimes by the vast majority of department's submitting as a policy success. The failure of police to identify hate crimes has downstream consequences because of the central role that police officers play in the investigation of hate crime. In jurisdictions where police officers report no hate crimes, it is hard to imagine that prosecutors will prosecute individuals for hate crime violations.

With respect to decisions about actual charges, as legal officials, it is the prosecutors' who play the most critical role. In thinking about hate crime charges, prosecutors must contend with a variety of variables not typically at issue in other crimes. One of these issues specifically of concern in hate crime cases is the reluctance of victims of particular backgrounds (gays, lesbians, persons who are transgender, African Americans, Latinos) to report, and later to interact with the police (Devine & Spellberg, 2009). Hate crimes statutes also require that the defendant's bias motivation that be proven, something that may be complicated if there are not hate symbols, slur or epithets, or other obvious indications of bias used in the crime (Devine & Spellberg, 2009). Prosecutors may be reluctant to bring hate crime charges because of the difficulty of proving the crime's motive, which is not a typical task for them.

Studies of prosecutor's decisions in hate crime cases support the idea that they are especially reluctant to bring charges in hate crime cases that for a variety of reasons that they may find difficult to win (Bell, 2002; Byers, Warren-Gordon, & Jones, 2011; Phillips, 2009). One analysis of the frequency of hate crime prosecutions as reported by the National Prosecutors Survey in 2001 found very little prosecution of hate crime, with nearly 78.2% of prosecutor's offices in states with a crime law indicating that they had not prosecuted a crime in the previous 12 months (Byers et al., 2012). Such a low level of prosecution did not appear in other specialized areas such as domestic violence, stalking, or child abuse cases.

Studies which ask prosecutors about their decision-making processes in hate crime cases have revealed that prosecutors view hate crime to be an area characterized by complexity and risk. McPhail and Jenness describe interviews with prosecutors in Texas who frequently mentioned the importance of decreasing the complexity of the case and minimizing risk. As one prosecutor they interviewed noted:

> When you make a decision to use hate crime law, you add to the complexity of the case. It's another element you must prove that you wouldn't have to prove otherwise. And you always run the risk of dividing a jury over that type of issue, so most prosecutors would decline to use it if the crime already had sufficient range of punishment. (McPhail & Jenness, 2005, p. 97)

Similarly, prosecutors "Center City" were asked about the appropriate types of cases for hate crime charges. Prosecutors were concerned that if they brought too many charges in cases that were not successful, they might create problems down the line – or "water down the law" (Bell, 2002). One ADA said:

> My feeling, my view, is that I try to make it traditional hate crime law so as not to lose its impact or power. I take cases that would be successful on the merits, not just add on significance. I don't want to water down the law. I reserved charging for the strong cases. (Bell, 2002, p. 165)

Prosecutors' reluctance in hate crime cases may be an appropriately cautious response to the difficulty of mounting a successful case (Bell, 2002; McPhail & Jenness, 2005). Though there are few, if any, nationwide empirical measures of how frequently prosecutors bring charges, one study of hate crime prosecutions examined cases referred by investigators for hate crime prosecutions in one New Jersey County between 2001 and 2004. Of the 23 cases for which Phillips had data, fewer than 50%, just 11 cases resulted in a criminal convictions, the most successfully prosecuted hate crime cases were those in which bias was the primary motivation (Phillips, 2009, p. 90).

PART III. HATE CRIME ENFORCEMENT AS A POLICY FAILURE?

Analysis of the public policy literature argues that the discussions of what constitutes policy failure may evaluate whether policies achieve their stated outcome or objective (McConnell, 2015). One of the many ways of measuring policy failure then is to assess the gap between the government's goals and measurable policy outcomes (McConnell, 2015). In the case of hate crime law, one important government goal would be to support hate crime victims by punishing those who commit hate crime. As the previous section shows, multiple studies of police and prosecutors in various locations around the United States suggest that hate crime law has not been adequately enforced. Hate crime law may, thus, be, at least initially, seen as a policy failure. This section will evaluate whether the "policy failure" label is truly appropriate in the case of hate crime law.

Hate Crimes in the Wake of the 2016 Presidential Election

Further evidence of policy failure in the area of hate crimes law appeared after the presidential election of Donald Trump. Trump had used racially divisive rhetoric on the campaign trail (Bell, 2019). In some cases, this rhetoric encouraged whites to attack minorities protesting at Trump rallies. The first hint that this affected hate crimes was that after the election of Donald Trump in November, several different organizations measuring hate crimes showed an increase in of hate crimes over the previous year (SPLC, 2019). The FBI statistics, which are generally the most conservative, demonstrated a modest increase in the number of hate crimes to 6,121, a 5-year high, and in increased of 5% from the figures in 2015. In 2017, FBI data showed a much larger increase in the number of hate crimes, a 17% increase in the number of hate crimes over the previous year (FBI, 2018). Research conducted 2 years after the election tracking hate crimes in the areas in which Trump held rallies found significant increases in the number of hate crimes. According to researchers, Feinberg, Regina Branton, and Valerie Martinez-Ebers, counties that hosted a rally by then-candidate Donald Trump saw a 226% increase in the number of recorded hate crimes (Feinberg et al., 2019).

Though the FBI statistics in the wake of the election showed relatively little increases in 2016, this was not true of other data. In fact, both the national and local advocacy groups ranging from the Anti-Defamation League (ADL) to the Southern Poverty Law Center (SPLC) have long tracked hate crimes. Reports collected by the SPLC showed much more dramatic increase in the number of hate crimes occurring in the wake of the election. In the 10 days following the election in 2016 SPLC received reports of 876 hate crimes occurring around the country (SPLC, 2016).[6]

Rating the National Temperature on Hate Crimes

Law enforcement officers' and prosecutors' reluctance to enforce hate crime law could possibly be sign from the American public of hesitancy regarding punishing outward expressions of racism. This is an important question, particularly in the wake of the 2016 election of Donald Trump, who used racist rhetoric during the campaign, yet still was able to win enough support to capture the presidency. Moreover, the rise in hate crimes documented by even conservative FBI figures suggests that large numbers of individuals remain committed to engaging in bias motivated behavior. The rally in Charlottesville in August 2017 and the targeting of university campuses by groups on the alt-right could suggest that Americans are no longer committed to a hate crime project. This section evaluates that the notion that the policy failure and the recent extremist activity of both suggestive of the fact that Americans do not support the enforcement are hate crime law.

The most systematic measure that exists regarding support for hate crime enforcement is polling data on hate crimes. Americans have long supported hate crime legislation, even before many states had a crime legislation. A Gallup poll of the US public conducted in February 1999 asked if the respondent supported, "harsher penalties for crimes motivated by hate of certain groups than penalties for the same crimes if they are not motivated by this kind of hate." Despite the fact that this was not an accurate description of hate crime legislation, which contains punishment for crimes based on particular types of motivation, as opposed to protecting particular groups, 70% of the individuals asked supported such legislation, while only 25% were opposed (Newport, 1999). Though support for hate crime legislation was lower among Republicans and conservatives, respondents overwhelmingly supported inclusion in hate crime legislation all groups they were asked about in the poll: "racial minorities, religious and ethnic minorities, women and homosexuals" (Newport, 1999).

A later Gallup poll in 2007 examined American support for the expansion of hate crime law into the area of gender identity. In that poll, 68% of respondents expressed support for hate crime laws that included the categories of sexual orientation and gender identity. Another poll also taken in 2007 was even more supportive of the strengthening of hate crime legislation in these categories. This 2007 Hart research poll demonstrated that "every major subgroup of the electorate – including traditionally conservative groups such as Republican men (56%) and evangelical Christians (63%)" were supportive of adding the categories of sexual orientation and gender identity to hate crime legislation (Newport, 2007).

There is also anecdotal evidence to suggest that many Americans reject both the ideology of white supremacy and the tactics of white supremacists. Americans around the United States expressed shock and outrage at the hate murders at a Pittsburgh synagogue in 2018 and the murder of activist Heather Heyer in Charlottesville, Virginia, in August 2017. Activists' intense responses to the Unite the Right rally in Charlottesville was another sign of a rejection of the white supremacist ideology. Events in Charlottesville suggest Americans resistance in the face of white supremacy. Thousands of anti-racist counterdemonstrators who gathered in Charlottesville on the day of the Unite the Right rally. These ranged from clergy members to armed anti-facists. They were joined by thousands of residents protesting, somewhat dwarfing the hundreds of far right protestors who came for the Unite the Right rally. President Trump's characterization of Charlottesville as a conflict involving violence on "both sides" was heavily criticized (Gray, 2019). The rejection of the message of white supremacy was also present in 2018 when hundreds of anti-racist demonstrators also turned up on the anniversary of the rally, greatly outnumbering the dozen far-right protestors.

There have also been smaller grassroots reactions attempting to engage the public in the hate crime project. In the wake of the election, a non-profit media organization Propublica engaged coalition of media organizations, with the "documenting hate" project. The aim of this endeavor was to increase reporting and documentation of hate crimes. Activists in states without hate crime legislation, or with poor hate crime legislation, campaigned for it's establishment. Legislators passed hate crime law in Indiana (a state which had none at all) and strengthened it in Utah, a state that had previously had poor hate crime legislation (Callahan, 2019; Roche, 2019).

CONCLUSION AND DISCUSSION

By all accounts, 30 years after the creation of hate crime law many American law enforcement and prosecutors have not been able to skillfully adapt to the significant challenges of investigating bias-motivated crime. Getting accurate numbers for instances of hate crimes is complicated. Victims are often reluctant to report hate crime. Police departments must devote special resources – including specialized units – to encourage reporting and investigation of bias-motivated incidents. The large number of police departments that report that no hate crime occurred in their cities, and evidence from around the country suggests that police have not risen to the challenge of fully enforcing hate crime law. Consequently, national numbers are suspect and hate crime is most likely under reported.

There are important implications of this failure for equity. Targets of hate crime are racial, ethnic, religious, sexual, and other minorities – those most vulnerable and marginalized in American society (see Table 3). And, of course, then, it is these groups who have the most to lose when enforcement and reporting of hate crimes fail.

Scholars write of the notion of "empathetic failure" – the failure to empathize with those who are different. Empathetic failures often result in discrimination. One might argue that the current state of hate crime law enforcement – police agencies across the country choosing not to participate in hate crime data collection, and 88% of police departments indicating that no hate crime occurred in their particular jurisdiction – is an example of empathetic failures. Thus, the circumstances this chapter detail how discrimination is compounded, resulting in neglect to stigmatized groups' harms, and an increase in aggression (Zaki & Cikara, 2015).

Yet, the failure of police departments to investigate hate crime and the failure of prosecutors to bring charges in all the cases which warrant it is complex. The ways that hate crime law operates, the organization of police departments and the diversity of the ways in which hate crime is processed in this country are reflective of systemic problems other than simple empathic failure. The structure of hate crime law itself creates difficulty for those charged with its enforcement. Some of this has to do with the ways in which hate crime law emerged in our federal system – most of the state legislation was created before federal legislation and activists in some states were able to push for and get passed earlier legislation that covered more categories. In other states, activists were not able to get hate crime law passed or once the state law was passed it was less inclusive than the federal legislation. A mismatch between the state and federal legislation creates ambiguity for law enforcement officers. In addition, law enforcement officers struggle with the difficulty of investigating not just who the perpetrator is, and what he or she did, but also why the perpetrator committed the crime.

This difficulty is magnified by the fact that many police departments have different structures for investigating hate crime. Some structures, such as the absence of a standalone unit entirely focused on hate crime, increase the difficulty that law enforcement officers face. Other departments have few resources to devote to hate crime and no policy to guide officers' decision-making.

Polling data demonstrating popular support for hate crime legislation fly in the face of the weak institutional response to hate crimes. In addition to polling data, there is also been significant grassroots mobilization – massive counter demonstrations, attempts to bolster hate crime legislation, and a willingness to convict hate murderers in response to white supremacist activity. Nonetheless, much hate crime remains uninvestigated, counted, and prosecuted. We do not know if there

Table 3. Hate Crime Statistics by Race.

	2008	2009	2010	2011	2012	2013	2014	2015	2016	2017
Total number of race crimes	4,934	4,057	3,949	3,645	3,467	3,563	3,227	4,216	4,426	5,060
Anti-White	829	668	697	593	763	754	734	789	909	864
Percentage of total (White)	16.80%	16.47%	17.65%	16.27%	22.01%	21.16%	22.75%	18.71%	20.54%	17.08%
Anti-Black	3,596	2,902	2,765	2,619	2,295	2,371	2,022	2,201	2,220	2,458
Percentage of total (Black)	72.88%	71.53%	70.02%	71.85%	66.20%	66.55%	62.66%	52.21%	50.16%	48.58%
Anti-Hispanic/Latino[a]	792	492	747	534	514	432	389	392	483	552
Percentage of total (Latino)	n/a	n/a	n/a	n/a	n/a	n/a	n/a	9.30%	10.91%	10.91%
Anti-Asian/Pacific Islander[b]	170	149	203	175	143	167	205	142	146	183
Percentage of Total (Asian)	3.45%	3.67%	5.14%	4.80%	4.12%	4.69%	6.35%	3.37%	3.30%	3.62%

Source: https://ucr.fbi.gov/hate-crime

[a]Hispanic/Latino was listed as an ethnicity – not a race – until 2015. Therefore, the proportion of hate crimes committed against Hispanics/Latinos cannot be calculated.
[b]Asian/Pacific Islanders were listed as the same category until 2013. In this chart, the counts of crimes against Asians and Pacific Islanders are combined for 2013 and after.

are data on which category of hate crimes is less likely to be investigated by the police and result in hate crime charges. These two factors, combined with the presence of police agencies that report increasingly large numbers of hate crime and prosecutors that insist on prosecution, it seems more appropriate to characterize the American approach to hate crime as a simple policy failure – many Americans want hate crime law to be enforced, but are unaware of the inadequacies of existing measures to address the problem. The existence of state and federal legislation, with jurisdictions committing different amounts of resources, creates patchwork of enforcement of hate crime legislation with different protections for those targeted by hate crime. Even in jurisdictions with hate crime law a close look at hate crime law enforcement has suggested, the hate crimes laws that we have in this country are structurally difficult to enforce for police and prosecutors.

Patchwork enforcement of law is of course characteristic of the American federal system. To the extent that activists dislike the fact that hate crimes victims in places like New York may receive more support than hate crime victims in Hawaii (a state that has never reported hate crimes to the FBI) now that the battle for state statutes has largely been won, more attention needs to be paid to the important axes of hate crime law enforcement – specifically police who investigate crime and prosecutors who decide to bring charges. These two agencies are the front lines in making hate crime.

There is also the issue of the resources most cities and towns are willing to invest in enforcing hate crime law. While the presence of hate crime law and police department's written hate crime policies are important (Johnson, 2019), one rarely emphasized issue is the need for dedicated institutions who are primarily responsible for hate crime. Specialized citywide police detective units provide more support for officers who may struggle with issues of classification (Bell, 2002; Cronin et al., 2007). Such units work on more hate crime cases and, therefore, develop expertise in the area. Similarly, prosecutors that specialize in hate crime prosecution will be able to develop expertise over time. Specialized detective units and prosecutors who specialize in the prosecution of hate crime require that jurisdictions devote special resources to hate crime. Because of policy failures depressing the number of hate crimes in most official numbers, officials may not see this as necessary. The current era of rising numbers of hate crime and increased white supremacist activity should suggest a more aggressive approach to the enforcement of hate crime law that can more appropriately support those targeted by hate crime.

NOTES

1. Both the NCVS and the FBI use the language from the Federal Hate Crime Statistics Act, which define hate crime as a crime: "motivated by bias against the victim due to his or her race, ethnicity, gender or gender identity, sexual orientation, religion or disability."

2. These statutes were created to address violence by the Ku Klux Klan.

3. These statutes punish the desecration of churches and other places of worship and cemeteries.

4. According to the Center for the Study of Hate and Extremism at California State University, San Bernardino, hate crime hoaxes are exceedingly rare, such that fewer than 1% of hate crimes reported to the police are false (Burch, 2019).

5. Cross burnings are not unusual in the context of hate crime cases. In other words, it is a type of crime officers trying to enforce hate crime legislation might encounter.

6. When evaluating whether a particular source of data, either FBI statistics or data gathered by advocacy groups like the Anti-Defamation League it is very important to consider the ways in which the statistics are created. The source of these statistics on hate crime vary. FBI statistics are generated by law enforcement agencies. Advocacy groups have a variety of ways of collecting accounts of incidents of hate crime. They may collect incidents from news reports. Advocacy groups may also receive reports from individuals who have experienced hate crime. In this way, advocacy statistics provide a sharp contrast with police statistics. This may explain, at least in part the difference between police statistics and the numbers of hate crimes collected by advocacy groups.

REFERENCES

Aldhous, P. (2018). The cities where the cops see no hate. *BuzzFeed News*, December 13. Retrieved from https://www.buzzfeednews.com/article/peteraldhous/hate-crimes-miami-police-irving-syracuse

Bell, J. (2002). *Policing hatred: Law enforcement, civil rights, and hate crime*. New York, NY: New York University Press.

Bell, J. (2009). Policing and surveillance. In F. M. Lawrence (Ed.), *Responding to hate crime* (pp. 89–108). Westport, CT: Prager.

Bell, J. (2013). *Hate thy neighbor: Move in violence and the persistence of racial segregation in American housing*. New York, NY: New York University Press.

Bell, J. (2019). The resistance and the stubborn person unsurprising persistence of hate and extremism in the United States. *Indiana Journal of Global Legal Studies*, *26*(1), 305–316.

Burch, A. D. S. (2019). Hate crime hoaxes are rare, but can be "devastating." *New York Times*, February 22, section A, p. 1.

Byers, B. D., Warren-Gordon, K., & Jones, J. A. (2012). Predictors of hate crime prosecutions: An analysis of data from the national prosecutors survey and state-level bias crime laws. *Race and Justice*, *2*(3), 203–219.

Boyd, E., Berk, R., & Hamner, K. (1996). 'Motivated by hatred or prejudice': Categorization of hate-motivated crimes in two police divisions. *Law & Society Review*, *30*(4), 819–850.

Callahan, R. (2019). Indiana governor signs hate crimes measure into law. *AP News*. Retrieved from https://www.apnews.com/939de847d4cf4d4086048b0c74170496

Center for the Study of Hate and Extremism. (2017). Final U.S. Status Report Hate Crime Analysis & Forecast for 2016/2017. Retrieved from https://csbs.csusb.edu/sites/csusb_csbs/files/Final%20Hate%20Crime%2017%20Status%20Report%20pdf.pdf

Cronin, S. W., McDevitt, J., Farrell, A., Nolan, J. J. III. (2007). Bias-crime reporting: Organizational responses to ambiguity, uncertainty, and infrequency in eight police departments. *American Behavioral Scientist, 51*(2), 213–231.

134 Cong Rec H 3373, vol. 134, no. 70. Hate Crimes Statistics Act. 100th Congress, 2nd Session Congressional Record. May 18, 1988. 134 Cong.

Devine, R. A., & Spellberg, A. J. (2009). Hate crime prosecution. In F. M. Lawrence (Ed.), *Responding to hate crime* (pp. 89–108). Westport, CT: Prager.

Feinberg, A., Regina, B., & Valerie, M. E. (2019). Counties that hosted a 2016 Trump rally saw a 226 percent increase in hate crimes. *The Washington Post* (Online), March 22. Retrieved from https://www.washingtonpost.com/politics/2019/03/22/trumps-rhetoric-does-inspire-more-hate-crimes/

Garafalo, J. (1991). Racially motivated crimes in New York City. In M. J. Lynch & E. B. Paterson (Eds.), *Race and criminal justice* (pp. 161–173). Albany, NY. Harrow and Heston.

Garafalo, J., & Martin, S. (1993). *Bias motivated crimes: Their characteristics and law enforcement response*. Carbondale, IL: Center for the Study of Crime Delinquency and Corrections.

Glickhouse, R. (2019). *5 Things you need to know about hate crimes in America*. New York, NY: ProPublica.

Gray, R. (2019). Trump defends white-nationalist protesters: 'Some very fine people on both sides'. *The Atlantic*, August 15, 2017. Retrieved from https://www.theatlantic.com/politics/archive/2017/08/trump-defends-white-nationalist-protesters-some-very-fine-people-on-both-sides/537012/

Haider-Markel, D. (1998). The politics of social regulatory policy: State and federal hate crime policy and implementation effort. *Political Research Quarterly, 51*(1), 69–88.

Jacobs, J. B., & Potter, K. (1998). *Hate crimes: Criminal law and identity politics.* Oxford: Oxford University Press.

Jenness, V., & Grattet, R. (2001). *Making hate a crime: From social movement to law enforcement.* London: Russell Sage Foundation.

Johnson, D. (2018). Report: Rise in hate violence tied to 2016 presidential election. Southern Poverty Law Center. Retrieved from https://www.splcenter.org/hatewatch/2018/03/01/report-rise-hate-violence-tied-2016-presidential-election

Johnson, W. (2019). The importance and structure of a written hate crime policy. *Police Chief, 86*(3), 30–34.

King, R. D. (2007). The context of minority group threat: Race, institutions, and complying with hate crime law. *Law & Society Review, 41*(1), 189–224.

Lieberman, M., & Freeman, S. (2009). Confronting violent bigotry: Hate crime laws and legislation. In F. M. Lawrence (Ed.), *Responding to hate crime* (pp. 1–30). Westport, CT: Prager.

Martin, S. E. (1995). 'A cross-burning is not just an Arson': Police social construction of hate crimes in Baltimore County. *Criminology, 33*(3), 303.

McConnell, A. (2015). What is policy failure? A primer to help navigate the maze. *Public Policy and Administration, 30*(3–4), 221–242.

McDevitt, J., Levin, J., & Bennett, S. (2002). Hate crime offenders: An expanded typology. *Journal of Social Forces, 58*(2), 303–317.

McPhail, B., & Jenness, V. (2005). To charge or not to charge? That is the question: The pursuit of strategic advantage in prosecutorial decision-making surrounding hate crime. *Journal of Hate Studies, 4*(1), 89.

McVeigh, R., Welch, M., & Bjarnason, T. (2003). Hate crime reporting as a successful social movement outcome. *American Sociological Review, 68*(6), 843–867.

Newport, F. (1999). One in four nonwhites worried about hate crime. *Gallup News Service,* February 23. Retrieved from https://news.gallup.com/poll/4057/one-four-nonwhites-worried-about-hate-crimes.aspx

Newport, F. (2007). Public favors expansion of law to include sexual orientation. *Gallup News Service,* May 17. Retrieved from https://news.gallup.com/poll/27613/public-favors-expansion-hate-crime-law-include-sexual-orientation.aspx

Nolan, J., & Akyama, Y. (2002). Assessing the climate for hate crime reporting in law enforcement organizations: A force field analysis. *The Justice Professional, 15*(2), 87–103.

Nolan, J. J, Haas, S. M., Turley, E., Stump, J., & LaValle, C.. (2015). Assessing the "statistical accuracy" of the national incident-based reporting system hate crime data. *American Behavioral Scientist, 59*(2), 1562–1587.

Pezzella, F. S., Matthew, F., & Keller, T. (2019). The dark figure of hate crime, underreporting. *American Behavioral Scientist,* 1–24.

Phillips, N. D. (2009). The limitations of the hate crime typology crimes in one New Jersey County between 2001 and 2004. *Journal of Interpersonal Violence, 24*(5), 883–905.

Roche, L. R. (2019). Hate crime bill signing ceremony in Utah Capitol marked by emotion, *Desert New,* April 2. Retrieved from https://www.deseretnews.com/article/900063571/utah-gov-gary-herbert-signs-hate-crime-bill.html

Southern Poverty Law Center. (2016). Ten days after: Harassment and intimidation in the aftermath of the election. Retrieved from https://www.splcenter.org/sites/default/files/com_hate_incidents_report_2017_update.pdf

U.S. Department of Justice, *Hate Crime Statistics,* 1992–2017. Retrieved from https://www.fbi.gov/services/cjis/ucr/hate-crime

Wolfe, Z. J. (2018). *Hate crimes law.* Minneapolis, MN: Thomson Reuters/West.

Zaki, J., & Cikara, M. (2015). Addressing empathic failures. *Current Directions in Psychological Science, 24*(6), 471–476. doi:10.1177/0963721415599978

CHAPTER 3

"YOU COMPLETE ME": BATMAN, JOKER, AND THE COUNTERSUBVERSIVE POLITICS OF AMERICAN LAW AND ORDER

Jeffrey R. Dudas

ABSTRACT

It is widely recognized by scholars that superhero stories tend to glorify vigilante justice; after all, these stories often maintain that extralegal acts of violence are necessary for combatting existential threats to personal and public safety. This scholarly common sense fosters a widespread dismissal of superhero stories as uncomplicated apologia for an authoritarian politics of law and order that is animated by hatred of unpopular people and ideas. However, some prominent contemporary Batman stories, including those told in the graphic novels of Grant Morrison and in the blockbuster movies of Christopher Nolan, are ambivalent: in their portraits of Batman and Joker as dark twins and secret colleagues, these stories both legitimize and challenge the countersubversive politics of American law and order.

Keywords: Law and popular culture; law and culture; law and order; superheroes; Batman; Joker

Studies in Law, Politics, and Society, Volume 85, 49–73
Copyright © 2021 by Emerald Publishing Limited
All rights of reproduction in any form reserved
ISSN: 1059-4337/doi:10.1108/S1059-433720210000085004

Criminals aren't complicated.

Batman, *The Dark Knight*

I could never kill you ...Where would the act be without my straight man?

Joker, *Batman and Son*

Between the idea and the reality of common meaning falls the shadow of the violence of the law, itself.

Robert Cover, "Nomos and Narrative"

1. INTRODUCTION

Modern law, according to Peter Fitzpatrick (1992), is mythologized as a double sign: it signifies both an enlightened polity that governs according to reason rather than desire *and* an empire of procedures that ensures that human passions are resisted in the name of fairness and justice. Modern law, accordingly, points both to enlightened human aspiration and mature social order (Fitzpatrick, 1992). Thus, does the mythology of modern law update and memorialize Aristotle's (1996) injunction that "the law is reason unaffected by desire" (p. 88).[1] It is unsurprising, then, that critics invest in legal officials, institutions, and procedures to curb the undemocratic practices of authoritarian and proto-authoritarian governing regimes (Lee, 2018, p. 1).[2] Animated by populist grievance and hatred of unpopular minorities, such regimes trade in the passions that modern law supposedly resists.

But, as Fitzpatrick also makes clear, modern law's constitutive boundaries – between reason and desire, order and chaos, knowledge and superstition, civilization and primitiveness – are themselves fictions.[3] Standing not on unbroken bedrock but rather atop an interlocking series of tectonic plates, modern legal actors and institutions are always and already exposed by, even as they furiously deny, the fractured ground beneath their feet. Indeed, modern law doesn't defeat desire, irrationality, and hatred; it instead represses those emotions, denies their constitutive influences on "enlightened" legal actors and institutions, and polices the imaginary, fictive boundaries on which the legitimacy derived from these repressions rests.[4] So it is, for example, that arguably the worst, most "irrational" excesses of today's most prominent proto-authoritarian regime – found in the Trump Administration's use of immigration politics to pursue white male supremacist fantasies of victimhood and redemption – have proceeded with the complicity of American legal officials, procedures, and institutions. Countersubversives all, purveyors of American "law and order" politics at once deny their exterminatory fantasies and project their own fears of boundary collapse onto actual victims of state violence such as non-violent criminal offenders (Alexander, 2010) and undocumented migrants (De León, 2015; Longazel, 2016).

Yet such undemocratic articulations of law and order are found not only in the words and actions of legal officials and the complicity of American institutions. For such authoritarian impulses to be intelligible – for them to translate into widely acceptable political practices in an ostensibly democratic society – they must also register in the domain of the popular.[5] More than just traces, in the prominent stories that transmit American popular culture can be found the echoes of our ongoing fascination with authoritarian politics and our broad willingness to accept, even demand, the countersubversive suspension of democratic values and practices in the name of law and order. But sometimes in those same stories can be found also an ambivalent response to the politics of law and order – a response that exposes and challenges the forms of subjection that those politics covet.

I will argue here that some of the most prominent recent entries in the super-hero genre (in the Batman universe, in particular) articulate America's contempo-rary countersubversive politics in ambivalent ways – in ways that both legitimize *and* challenge reigning American practices of law and order. It is, of course, widely recognized that superhero stories tend to glorify vigilante justice; after all, these stories often maintain that extralegal acts of violence are necessary for combatting existential threats to personal and public safety. In fact, such recogni-tion amounts to a scholarly common sense that has led to widespread dismissal of superhero stories as little more than apologia for authoritarian politics – as simplistic, relentlessly anti-law stories, I mean.[6] In the parlance of modern law, superhero stories revive pre-modern, primitive visions of order; they articulate, as Bainbridge (2015) summarizes, "the perfect revenge/control fantasy; power with-out the constraint of law" (p. 747).

But to insist, as I do here, that modern law *represses* rather than overcomes its constitutive desires complicates matters. Foregrounding the countersubver-sive character of modern law makes clear that the desires and fears that animate contemporary American law and order politics are not at war with modern law's pretentions toward reason; they are, instead, immanent, essential features of law's claims to be "reason unaffected by desire" (Ewick, 2013). Unsurprisingly, then, at least some contemporary superhero stories – which depict the alliance of super heroic, autonomous will with formal legal authority – are also adept at exposing and interrogating the hatreds that modern law represses, thus, calling into question the legitimacy of American law and order itself.

In particular, contemporary Batman stories, which develop one of the old-est and most popular of America's superhero universes, illustrate this ambiva-lence. I will analyze two recent, critically and commercially successful Batman stories: writer Grant Morrison's 2006–2013 run in the pages of DC Comics and 2008's blockbuster movie *The Dark Knight*. Each of these texts portrays Gotham City's formal institutions of law enforcement as incapable of warding off sub-versive, existential threat. In need of Batman's extralegal vigilantism, Gotham City's unofficial partnership with Batman (exemplified by the friendships between Batman, Gotham Police Commissioner James Gordon and, in *The Dark Knight*, Gotham District Attorney Harvey Dent) legitimizes an undemocratic politics of law and order.

And, yet, these same texts also highlight Joker, who is both arguably the most iconic villain in American popular culture and a character who illuminates in manifold ways how contemporary American law and order politics represses, projects, and demonizes – but never overcomes – the base desires and fears that constitute it. Joker is, in fact, a liminal figure who exposes the instability of the boundaries – between reason and desire, order and chaos, and civilization and primitiveness – that distinguish law as an organizing force in modern times. Joker is Batman's dark twin; his presence threatens a boundary collapse that exposes Batman's own liminality and, thus, makes clear how Batman's vigilantism at once supports *and* challenges the legitimacy of Gotham law and order. Never able to overcome his dark twin, who infamously returns after every defeat, the best that Batman can do is repress Joker in Arkham Asylum and, so, temporarily shore up the boundaries that the clown's liminality articulates. Thus, it is that, just as the legitimacy of modern law simultaneously relies upon and is threatened by the repressed "wild beasts" of human desire, so too does Batman's countersubversive heroism depend not upon killing Joker but upon repressing the illicit, destructive desires that Joker personifies and which Batman secretly shares.

2. MODERN LAW'S COUNTERSUBVERSIVE AUTOBIOGRAPHY

The mythology of modern law insists (against its own repressions) that legal actors and institutions protect societies from the ever-present, but destructive tendencies of human desire – which is associated with pre-modern, primitive, subversive forces. Accordingly, to take modern law's self-portrait seriously requires that we interrogate the "countersubversive" purpose that it claims for itself. And to do this is, in part, to embed contemporary American law and order within a national tradition of countersubversive politics – a politics that fixates on the alleged threats that unpopular people and ideas present to personal and public safety. Treating law's countersubversive autobiography leads us to spotlight how modern legal actors and institutions are obsessed not with justice and fairness but rather with the demonic forces that supposedly portend their obliteration. Locating existential, subversive threat at the political and social margins, America's law and order acolytes imagine themselves as defenders of core, "mainstream" values and "ordinary" people and ways of life that are under assault from savage, devouring forces bent on exterminatory violence. "The label countersubversive," according to its foremost chronicler Michael Rogin (1987), "points to the fact that the important bearers of American political demonology have not been extremists or subversives, but their foes" (p. 274).

Crucially, the American countersubversive worldview developed in relation to European contact with non-white, indigenous peoples, on one hand, and African slavery, on the other hand. Resulting, predictable conflicts of interest over resources, authority, and freedom in the "New World" – conflicts over the conventional interest-based matters of politics, I mean – were accompanied by white fantasies "about peoples of color [that] exposed and intensified actual conflicts of interest" such that those "interests and fantasies could neither be reduced to nor separated from one another" (Rogin, 1987, p. 277).[7] Thus were conflicts over "frontier" land and authority, for example, accompanied by frequently apocryphal depictions of "primitive," bloodthirsty Indians whose savagery justified both atrocities committed by individual whites and the systematic acts of governmental expropriation that marked the era of Indian removal (see generally, Rogin, [1975] (1991); Slotkin, [1973] (2000)). Similarly, American white supremacists of all eras have imagined themselves the potential and actual victims of demonic black power and domination (which is frequently sexual in character) – a view that allows them to evade responsibility for, and justify, both the actual power dynamics of American slavery and the contemporary, reverberating impacts of those dynamics (Jordan, 1968, generally; Slotkin, [1985] (1998), pp. 227–241; Rogin, 1987, pp. 190–235). A patchwork quilt made up of interest-based calculations, on one hand, and race-based fantasies, on the other hand: the American countersubversive tradition encourages a politics that transforms "interest conflicts into psychologically based anxieties over national and American identity." Countersubversives thus inflate political opponents into all-consuming threats and political differences become "absolute struggles between good and evil" (Rogin, 1987, pp. 68, 58).

The specific process according to which American countersubversives inflate cultural difference into subversive threat and demonize those marked by difference as existential, exterminatory terrors mimics the splitting process that is characteristic of early childhood experience and ego development. Rogin thus theorized the American countersubversive worldview by employing the tools of Kleinian psychoanalysis – a variant of the Freudian tradition that explores the primal mother–infant relationship. Parasitically dependent upon the maternal body for physical life in the same way that countersubversives depend upon subversives for psychic life (for identity), infants tend to develop the same paranoid fantasies of domination and persecution that infuse the countersubversive worldview.

Specifically, Melanie Klein argued that infants develop ego permanence by identifying and "introjecting" external objects into their imaginations. The most important of these objects is the mother, who the infant objectifies by "splitting" into a good and bad breast, imagining that they both dominate the breast and are persecuted by its apparent refusal (or inability) to serve as perpetual nourishment. According to Klein, healthy ego development depends upon the guilt that the infant feels for desiring the destruction of the hated "bad" part of the introjected object; for the infant fears that their exterminatory desire will result, as if by magic, in the loss of the loved "good" part of the object as well. Thus, does guilt over its homicidal desires compel the infant to psychic acts of "reparation," wherein the good and bad are integrated and the introjected object (mother) is recognized as a singular, human subject (Klein, 1975, pp. 306–313; see also Kristeva, 2001, pp. 74–76). The process of reparation ushers infants into the "depressive position,"[8] wherein early idealizations and fantasies give way to reality testing and, eventually, to healthy self-identifications with the external world (Klein, 1986, pp. 52–54).[9]

Stalled, disturbed ego development, on the other hand, leads to the infant self-getting stuck in the splitting phase, which fosters a "paranoid–schizoid" personality that is characterized by harsh, Manichean boundary drawing and maintenance that expels the "bad" and idealizes the "good" aspects of the introjected object. Regular oscillation between the depressive and paranoid–schizoid positions is, Klein thought, a normal feature of human life (Rollin, 1994, pp. 9–10); but prolonged immersion in the paranoid–schizoid position points to a disturbed worldview that compulsively splits the world into "good," favored objects and people and "bad," persecutory and existentially threatening objects to which the self is always vulnerable (Klein, 1986, p. 54).[10] Good and bad must, thus, be kept hermetically sealed from one another; although both are necessary, constituent parts of the introjected object(s) upon which association with the external world depends, the disturbed self insists that they are exact opposites and that the (fictional) boundaries between them are impermeable, if always vulnerable to breakdown.[11] And the more keenly that the paranoid–schizoid self feels the intimacy between good and bad (and thus its own vulnerability), the more extreme will be its desires to exterminate the bad, demonized object before it can itself be obliterated. At the core of this disturbed worldview, accordingly, are hysterical fears over the ever-present possibility of boundary collapse and the merger of self and other. Yet, the disturbed self also, paradoxically and secretly, desires exactly such a collapse and merger – for even the paranoid–schizoid recognizes on a sub-conscious level, and despite his or her characteristic protestations, that self and other *are* intimately related to one another. Thus are the favored and despised objects, people, forces, and/or ideas – the good and the bad, the included and the excluded, the self and the other – twinned, mirrored images of one another.[12]

I appreciate that wary readers may at this point throw up their hands in frustration. What do nearly century-old theories of ego development in infants have to do with modern law's autobiography, with the character of contemporary American law and order politics, and with the relationship between fictional comic book characters? Worse still, even if there is a connection between method and substance, doesn't this sort of theorization simply revive old, rightly-discarded reductions of complicated human behavior to simple, universal psychological drives? Isn't this all a bridge too far?

The problem is this: the splitting of introjected objects into supposedly pure categories of good and evil; identification with these split objects as the source of ego permanence (identity); the compulsive maintenance of the fictional boundaries occasioned by splitting, even amid paradoxical fears and desires of transgression; and the characteristic resort to exterminatory violence in response to the threats of the split-off, demonized, evil "other": this describes *exactly* the discursive process that animates modern law's countersubversive story of self. It is the *precise* method according to which the forces of law and order seek to carry out modern law's injunction to be "reason [good] unaffected by desire [evil]" and, thus, protect humans from our own split-off, "wild" desires (Aristotle, 1996, p. 88). Indeed, as a story of countersubversive purpose, the mythology of modern law is "dominated by splitting, by anxiety about boundary breakdown, and by invasive, devouring exterminatory enemies" (Rogin, 1987, p. 292). Modern law's *own autobiography* thus confesses that it is stuck in the paranoid–schizoid phase of ego development. And so the point is not to condemn America's law and order countersubversives as personally disturbed (though some of them may be, of course) but rather to show how they "share a disturbed ideology that functions as psychological protection." Precisely because it articulates modern law's story of self, the American discourse of law and order "convicts itself of psychological disturbance" (Rogin, 1987, pp. 292, 285).

This disturbance, I have intimated, is apparent in arguably the most prominent of contemporary American law and order practices: state violence directed against undocumented migrants (Gottschalk, 2015, pp. 215–240). Indeed, America's countersubversive politics turn desperate migrants into racialized, subversive others who simultaneously threaten (and thus preserve) valued American identities and act as containers for countersubversive fantasies of domination and persecution. Migrants are at once dismissed as primitive others to the American nation (they are "unskilled laborers") *and* inflated into all-consuming, devouring cancers on an otherwise healthy political body (they are "rapists," "drug dealers," "animals," and "terrorists" (Korte & Gomez, 2018) who inhabit "diseased" bodies (Turesky, 2018) that threaten "beautiful" American communities with dismembering gang violence (Phippen, 2017); or else they are thieves who "steal" American jobs. Either way, the literal and metaphoric border crossing of undocumented migrants threatens boundary collapse and, thus, justifies the exact exterminatory, dismembering violence of which the migrants themselves are accused.[13]

It is unsurprising that the countersubversive politics of undocumented migration register in the domain of law and order. For, just as the mythology of modern law would have it, "law and order" is offered as the bulwark of stability – as guardian of the always vulnerable borders between reason and desire, self and other. The forces of law and order are thus said to make up a "big, beautiful wall" that protects American selves from the alien invasions of countersubversive fantasy (Khan, Sands, &Turner, 2018).

Widely shared fears of border crossing and boundary collapse, and the hysterical invocations of law and order that express those fears, thus, animate contemporary American migration politics. As such, these politics are enmeshed within a distinctive tradition of American countersubversion that intersects rationality and fantasy in ways that compromise modern law's Aristotelean promise that it is "reason unaffected by desire." And, in this way, modern law points less to an enlightened universe of collective aspiration and more to a murky underworld of intersubjective fever dream.

To further investigate this fever dream – and its American analogue, the countersubversive politics of law and order[14] – let us turn now to mass, popular culture. For it is here, in the products of popular culture, where we find the less benighted and honorable "discourses of [our] present and past" (Hall, 1997, p. 291) and, in so doing, dredge up the raw, frequently disavowed materials out of which we make sense of ourselves and our world.[15] Identities, such as those spawned by the countersubversive worldview, are found here; so too, accordingly, are the "ideologies, fantasies, and unconscious desires that support" (Aristodemou, 2014, p. 3) and, in the ambivalent relationship between two of our most iconic fictional characters, challenge America's contemporary politics of law and order.

3. THE DARK TWINS OF GOTHAM LAW AND ORDER

Batman's ... general function is to police the conceptual walls at the boundaries of the civilized state: he climbs over them rather than breaks them down, and protects them as the Dark Knight.

Thomas Giddens, "Natural Law and Vengeance"

Loosen up, tight ass!

Joker, *Arkham Asylum*

Over the previous decade a burgeoning scholarship has interrogated the intersections between law and popular culture. As Sarat (2011) notes, this scholarship points not to the conventional law and society distinction between "law on the books" and "law in action" but instead toward an examination of "law in the image" (p. 3). Or, more precisely, the most compelling of this scholarship traces how reigning portraits of law in mass culture are at once reflections, distortions, and, because general publics rely upon such "mediated images and cultural products" for their understandings of how law works (Sarat & Scheingold, 2008, p. 3)[16], constitutive "agents" of both formal legal texts and articulate legal behavior (Manderson, 2011, p. 27; see also Haltom & McCann, 2008; McCann & Haltom, 2004, pp. 183–226, generally; Dudas, 2017, pp. 140–148; Nielsen, Patel, & Rosner, 2013).

According to Mezey (2011), this relationship among the legal word, the legal act, and the (popular) legal image is one of *translation*. Popular images of law, she argues, are not accurate reproductions of formal legal process so much as they are translations of widespread, enduring concerns about law into alternative domains of knowledge. Especially prominent in this regard are anxieties over the standards according to which modern law is legitimized as a society's primary organizing force. Popular culture texts, indeed, "ensure ... the afterlife of a central idea or anxiety within law by ritualizing and rethinking the problem through the lens of a different interpretive method" (Mezey, 2011, p. 70). Popular culture storytelling is fertile ground for the presentation of anxieties about modern law precisely because those anxieties, and the illicit desires to which they point, are routinely "suppressed in legal discourse" (Mezey, 2011, p. 68). Compulsively formalized, modern legal discourse is uptight, its authors desperate to repress the desires that constitute law itself (Goodrich, 1995, pp. 1052–1055; see also Cover, 1975, 1986).

Foremost among such anxieties are widespread concerns that due process of the law – the organization and execution of the state's punitive capacity according to procedures that treat the accused as rights-bearing subjects – does not produce substantively just outcomes.[17] Indeed, popular desire for vigilantism is, according to Smith (2019), most pronounced in societies where due process of the law is most strongly touted and celebrated. But vigilantism is not simply about justice; its "extra-legal punishment" is also about vengeance (Smith, 2019, p. 4). As such, vigilantism points not simply to desires for justice but also to desires to violently obliterate the perceived sources of transgression. Ironically, popular fantasies of vigilante justice (such as those frequently celebrated in superhero stories[18]) thus gesture not to popular rejection of law's promise to be reason free from desire but rather to widespread belief in employing exterminatory desire in the name of reason, which will then secure the very justice that law promises.

Accordingly, it is unsurprising that hysteria over the collapse of modern law's constitutive boundaries – the very boundaries from which, on the one hand, its popular legitimacy is derived and, on the other hand, which prompt anxiety and illicit desire for exactly such a collapse – is frequently translated into the realm of popular culture storytelling. And the Batman universe – an 80-year old storytelling domain that is rich enough to be considered a folk tradition, with each new generation of creators employing Gotham's unique settings and characters to render in fiction the major concerns of their times (Weldon, 2016) – proves to be well suited for the telling of these stories. Indeed, on the one hand, Batman is a "profoundly modern" character, a "quintessentially modern guardian" who employs reason, deduction, and logic to pursue justice (Giddens, 2015, pp. 769, 771). But, on the other hand, he is a highly skilled dispenser of a savage violence that leaps beyond the bounds of formal legal procedure; Batman, after all, characteristically disregards such entrenched legal conventions as due process and the rights of the accused. At once a cerebral, rational private detective and a frighteningly unhinged warrior[19] driven by guilt over the murder of his parents, and an associated desire for vengeance, Batman is a prototypical American countersubversive. A popular culture avatar of the American politics of law and order, Batman's vigilantism polices and strategically exploits the exact boundary of reason and desire that makes up, and legitimates, modern law.

And, although the Batman universe is populated by a myriad of well-known super villains, Joker is both Batman's original nemesis (he appeared in April 1940 in the pages of *Batman* #1) and arguably the most popular and influential villain in the history of American popular culture (Peaslee & Weiner, 2015). Creators in every genre of the Batman universe (comics, novels, movies, television serializations, and video games) have long understood the pride of place that Joker holds in the tradition; no new interpretation of the Batman universe is complete without an extended Joker storyline. Moreover, Batman's portrayal over the last 80 years has undergone significant shifts in tone; each of these shifts correspond with mirrored shifts in Joker's character. From an original "golden era" of stylish, noir-influenced storytelling to a "silver age" of hallucinatory, science fiction-influenced tales to the Warhol-esque, Pop Art stories associated with the original Batman TV series to the urban avenger, "Dark Knight" revivals of the 1980s and 1990s (featured in the "graphic novels" of Frank Miller and the movies of Tim Burton) to, finally, the contemporary, post-9/11 stories most prominently associated with Grant Morrison and Christopher Nolan and which are under examination in this essay: in each era, alterations in the character of Batman are matched, or *perhaps instigated*, by parallel changes in Joker's character.

Morrison's two-part 2008 story *Last Rites*, which breaks down the "fourth wall" of storytelling by imagining that Batman actually experienced each of these varied and contradictory *non-fictional* eras of storytelling, summarizes the historically symbiotic relationship between Batman and Joker, even as it insists that Joker is the active agent of change. Homicidal mastermind in the Golden Age, mad scientist and bio-terrorist in the Silver Age, "Pop Criminal" and mostly harmless prankster in the Pop Art era, sadistic purveyor of "wanton cruelty" in the Dark Knight era, nihilistic terrorist in the contemporary, post 9/11 era: Joker "keeps coming back … different," concludes Bruce Wayne. Cueing readers to the market demands of folk story-telling traditions, where iconic characters require constant refreshing, Morrison has Wayne realize that Joker "recreates himself constantly. Like some sort of super-MPD [multiple personality disorder]" (Morrison, 2008a). Morrison thus makes clear that shifts in the portrayal of Batman are actually *responses* to prior shifts in the portrayal of Joker; as a prototypical countersubversive, Batman employs increasingly brutal and arbitrary measures to combat the evolving threats presented by Joker.

Joker is, accordingly, the ur-subversive of the Batman universe; he is the dark twin over whom the countersubversive Batman obsesses, furiously denies his own resemblance to, demonizes, and continually represses but never overcomes. Thus was Morrison traversing the same countersubversive terrain as was Christopher Nolan in *The Dark Knight*, when he had Heath Ledger's Joker confess to Batman that "you complete me" (Nolan, 2008).[20] But Morrison's presentation of the "Batman of Zur-en-Arrh" in his 2009 story *Batman R.I.P.* exposes, as does *The Dark Knight* itself, the irony of Joker's confession. For it is not Batman who "completes" Joker, but exactly the opposite. As our hero's dark twin, Joker is, in fact, an essential part of Batman; he is a projection of Batman's repressed desires for savage vengeance.

The Batman of Zur-en-Arrh

Morrison's multi-year storyline began in 2007s *Batman and Son* with Batman tossing Joker's limp body (the Clown Prince of Crime has been shot in the face by a Batman imposter) into a Gotham dumpster. The dumpster is covered, as are a great number of Gotham's public spaces, in a mysterious graffito that reads "Zur-en-Arrh." But our hero pays no mind to these inscrutable messages. For, with Joker's return to Arkham Asylum, Batman has, in league with Commissioner Gordon, concluded a highly productive run over the previous months; together they have struck an apparently decisive blow in Gotham's war against crime (Morrison, 2007b).

But Batman has ignored the graffiti at his own peril. It turns out that the "Zur-en-Arrh" inscriptions are subliminal messages that have been implanted throughout the city by a new nemesis, Dr Simon Hurt – a shadowy figure who dresses, as if in a masquerade version of the Dark Knight himself, in black cape and exaggerated domino mask. Hurt leads the "Black Glove" – an international group of powerful, corrupt figures (dictators, religious leaders, Tech CEO's, and entertainment moguls) who gather periodically to engage in high-stakes betting over scenarios that Hurt has masterminded. His current wager is that he can destroy Batman once and for all, thereby completing a quest that has consistently frustrated Gotham's super villains. And Dr Hurt has a secret weapon aiding him in his nefarious plot. Not only does Hurt know Batman's secret identity; he promises the Black Glove that he holds "the keys to Bruce Wayne's mind" and that, accordingly, he will destroy Batman by rending Wayne's very identity.

Readers learn in 2008s *The Black Glove* that Dr Hurt was once affiliated with the American defense industry; he conducted sensory deprivation experiments for the military. We also learn that Batman had volunteered to undergo exactly this experiment. Desperate to figure out what motivated his greatest foe, Joker, Batman agreed to spend 10 days in Hurt's isolation chamber; Batman hoped that a deep dive into his own personality, experiences, and motivations would yield insight into Joker. Batman's gambit failed; he emerged from isolation with no greater understanding of Joker. But Batman's isolation did lead to Hurt developing a treasure trove of information about him: Hurt learned Batman's secret identity; he learned the original trauma and desire for vengeance that motivates the

Caped Crusader; and he developed a comprehensive understanding of Batman's previous adventures. Dr Hurt comes to believe that the key to destroying Bruce Wayne's mind (and thus the Batman identity that he developed) is to force him to relive, as if in an infinite loop, the primal trauma of his life: the murder of his parents, Thomas and Martha Wayne, on the streets of Gotham when Bruce was 8 years old. So during the isolation experiment Hurt implants the phrase "Zur-en-Arrh" in Batman's mind as a post-hypnotic trigger that is intended to return Bruce Wayne to, and confine him in, his own personal hell (Morrison, 2008b).

Its outlines sketched in *Batman and Son* and *The Black Glove*, Dr Hurt's plan comes to fruition in 2009s *Batman R.I.P.* (Morrison, 2009). In that story Hurt assembles an international "club of villains" (featuring such new villains as El Bossu, Scorpiana, and El Sombrero) to infiltrate Wayne manor and the Bat Cave, assault an increasingly paranoid and unstable Batman (who is, in fact, unhinged by Hurt's subliminal warfare), and shoot him full of illicit drugs (including "weapons grade crystal meth" and "street heroin"). Reduced to bare life, his Batman identity apparently damaged beyond repair, Bruce Wayne is deposited, unconscious and strung out, in the Gotham slums. A confident Dr Hurt and the villains subsequently infiltrate and seize control of Arkham Asylum. Convening the members of the Black Glove for the final event (the "danse macabre"), they await Bruce Wayne's inevitable arrival – after which they will bury him alive, do away with Batman forever, and (with help both from plants within the GCPD and Gotham's corrupt mayor) bring the city "to its knees."

So confident is Dr Hurt in Batman's coming demise that he has Joker freed from the asylum. Hurt plans to have Joker welcome Batman "home" (in a reprise of Joker's hosting of Batman in Morrison's 1989 graphic novel *Arkham Asylum*) and, then, in a show of his own villainous superiority, have Joker witness the death of Batman – a feat that Joker himself could never accomplish. But Dr Hurt has made two major, interconnected mistakes: he has, on the one hand, under-estimated both Batman and Joker and, on the other hand, he has fundamentally misunderstood the nature of their relationship. Hurt's errors lead not only to the failure of his plan to kill Batman and make Joker witness it; they also lead to his own demise at the hands of Joker, who eventually murders every member of the Black Glove before, in the pages of Morrison's later *Batman and Robin*, poisoning Hurt with Joker venom and burying him alive in Wayne Manor cemetery.

Dr Hurt's mistakes begin with the failure of his isolation chamber trigger: "Zur-en-Arrh." Hurt intended the phrase to evoke primal trauma and emotional ruin; but Bruce Wayne subsequently discovers that it has been implanted in his mind and, unbeknownst to Hurt, resignifies it be a source of strength. "Zur-en-Arrh" still triggers a return to Bruce Wayne's childhood trauma; but rather than paralyzing him it instead calls forth an emergency "back-up identity." Leaning into Bruce Wayne's hyper-rational tendencies, Morrison shows Batman antici-pating an attack on his mind and preparing for the bare life scenario that would result. Accordingly, in this emergency state, where Wayne imagines that he will lose his reason, he becomes the Batman of Zur-en-Arrh (Zur-en-Arrh is an imaginary world that Batman hallucinated once while under the influence of Professor Milo's "gas weapon"). Shorn of reason, the Batman of Zur-en-Arrh is a "streamlined engine, a silver bullet" who operates on pure instinct and a savage violence that is unrestrained even by the occasional taboos that Batman follows. The Batman of Zur-en-Arrh is thus dissociated from Bruce Wayne's reason – the last remnants of which are, in this emergency state, represented by an imaginary "alien hyper-imp" from the 5th dimension, "Bat-Mite." Bat-Mite hovers over Bruce's shoulder and periodically offers understanding and logic to the Batman of Zur-en-Arrh; but he also disappears at crucial moments (such as when the Batman of Zur-en-Arrh is preparing to confront Dr Hurt in Arkham Asylum).

Thus, as Hurt prepares Arkham to receive what he presumes will be a wasted foe, Bruce Wayne has roused himself into a half-lucid state and begun his transformation into the Batman of Zur-en-Arrh. In a vagrant's shopping cart that he has pre-planted in "Crime Alley" (the location of his parents' murder), Bruce finds needle and thread, tattered cloth, an apparently broken transistor radio, and a baseball bat. In short order, he sews a Batman costume, cape, and cowl; the colors are bright and garish, a telling mélange of purple, red, and yellow. Bruce fixes the radio – which becomes the "Bat Radia" and emits a signal that communicates with the Bat Computer in Wayne's Gotham penthouse and which will eventually be employed to override Arkham's security systems and wrest back control of the asylum from Dr Hurt. And, finally, the baseball bat becomes the Batman of Zur-en-Arrh's primary weapon (he becomes another type of bat-man); with it he will savagely assault a number of low-level Gotham criminals as he seeks the information that will lead him to confront Dr Hurt in Arkham.

Understand: the Batman of Zur-en-Arrh – Bruce Wayne without his reason – appears in Joker colors, mimics Joker's characteristic manipulation of the lines of communication, and uses blunt instruments to mercilessly assault his enemies, just as Joker infamously murdered the second Robin (Jason Todd) with a crowbar in 1988s *A Death in the Family* (Starlin, Aparo, & DeCarlo, 1988). The point is clear: if the Batman of Zur-en-Arrh is Bruce Wayne without his reason, then Bruce Wayne without his reason is none other than Joker himself. Unsurprising, then, that when Joker and the Batman of Zur-en-Arrh meet in Arkham, Joker immediately recognizes the transformation: "Oh you ... you turn up dressed like a clown. You look ... vulnerable." In his moment of greatest need, his identity under attack, Batman turns into Joker – whose instincts and terrifying brutality save both him and Gotham from Hurt's plan. Morrison makes the boundary collapse complete when he has artist Tony Daniel show the Batman of Zur-en-Arrh and Joker in combat, their bodies blending into one another.

Morrison thus understands that the Batman/Joker dynamic points to the exact parasitic, introjected self-other relationship that also tethers American countersubversives to their alien, subversive twins. Dr Hurt, though, has misjudged matters altogether; rather than a mortal enemy, Joker is the secret, primal source of Batman's strength.[21] Their relationship is symbiotic; just as in the case of American countersubversives and subversives, neither can exist without the other. And, so, Joker not only refuses to assist Hurt in his scheme to kill Batman; he actively undermines the plan by maiming several members of the club of villains (Joker disfigures El Bossu and lynches El Sombrero – "What *is* it about the *sombrero*? Some things are just *naturally* funny"). And then, having figured out its latent powers, Joker appears to activate the Bat-Radia himself, thus, trapping Hurt, the club of villains, and the members of the Black Glove in Arkham and turning them into Batman's prey: "the *black glove* quivering in an *insane asylum ... exactly* where he wants you." Indeed, having recovered his reason and returned to his conventional Batman identity, the Dark Knight and his allies foil the plan of Hurt – who beats a hasty, if temporary, retreat.

Joker never explicitly allies with Batman in the protracted battle against Dr Hurt (which spans exactly 50 issues and multiple, intertwined story lines); but he does help in his own ways. Joker, for example, eventually murders every member of the Black Glove in darkly comic ways; and then he does what Bruce Wayne's taboo on murder prevents him from doing: he poisons the evil doctor with Joker venom and buries him alive, rictus grin intact, in Wayne Manor cemetery. Showing an indifference for Hurt's fate that is unusual, Batman notes without disapproval that Joker has "dealt with" Hurt (Morrison, 2011b). Readers understand, as does Bruce, that Dr Simon Hurt, unlike all of Gotham's other supervillains, will not resurface.[22]

Joker in a Batman disguise, the unhinged Batman of Zur-en-Arrh at once personifies Bruce Wayne's forbidden desire for the savage violence, vengeance, and unrestrained freedom that characterize Joker's madness *and* illustrates just how quickly the scant distance between Joker's madness and Bruce Wayne's reason can be traversed. This latter dynamic, the intimacy of Batman and Joker, is, of course, a recurring theme in contemporary renditions. It is an intimacy that is often depicted (as it was in Grant Morrison's earlier *Arkham Asylum*) as repressed homoerotic attraction.[23] Indeed, in *Arkham Asylum*, Morrison and McKean (1989) have Joker refer to Batman as "dear" and "honey pie" – all the while imploring "Bats," with his "tight ass," to "loosen up" and let go of the reason that represses his desire for vengeance.

In the Batman of Zur-en-Arrh storyline under examination here, however, Morrison mutes the homoerotic notes of his earlier portrayals. Instead, Morrison is interested in boundary collapse and the furious maintenance that is required to (always temporarily) stave it off; his story line exposes just how precarious and unstable the (fictional) boundaries are between Batman's rationality and his madness – both of which, it turns out, are essential to Gotham law and order. The coalition of reason and desire that Batman employs to protect his city is expressed in the "first truth" of Batman's inextricable, if repressed and denied, association with Joker. A countersubversive champion of Gotham law and order, the vigilante Batman is thus a "quintessentially modern guardian" who polices the "conceptual walls at the boundaries of the civilized state" (Giddens, 2015, pp. 771, 774). But, like all American countersubversives, Batman's obsessive defense of the civilized state – his defense, I mean, of modern law's pretentions to being an empire of "reason unaffected by desire" – is betrayed by the affiliation of his own hidden desires with those of his subversive dark twin, a "murdering psychopath" who seeks to blow Gotham "half to hell."

When the chips are down, these "civilized" people ... they'll eat each other.

Joker, *The Dark Knight*

Christopher Nolan's *The Dark Knight* (*TDK*) was the highest-grossing motion picture of 2008, in both the United States and international markets (Box Office Mojo, 2008a). Unadjusted for inflation, it is the 10th highest-grossing movie of all time (Box Office Mojo, 2008b). The film is regularly lauded, as it was recently by the sports and popular culture website *The Ringer*, as the greatest superhero movie of all time (The Ringer, 2018).

More than just a commercially successful genre film, *TDK* was a critical juggernaut. It was nominated for eight Academy Awards in 2009; it won two, including a posthumous Best Supporting Actor that went to Heath Ledger for his portrayal of Joker (Box Office Mojo, 2009). *TDK* holds a "fresh score" of 94 on the review aggregator website *Rotten Tomatoes*, which indicates that 94% of all published reviews were positive. It was by this measure the most critically lauded movie of 2008, besting such critics' darlings as *The Wrestler*, *Milk*, and *Slumdog Millionaire* (Rotten Tomatoes, 2008).

A towering commercial and critical achievement, *TDK* redefined the possibilities of superhero movies; it dispensed of the silly elements formerly associated with the genre, highlighting instead the psychological complexity and gothic horror that had been the dominant themes of graphic superhero novels (both within, and apart, from the Batman universe) since the 1980s. It is not too much to say that *TDK* sits at the leading edge of Hollywood's contemporary employment of superhero stories (along with their close cousins, fantasy and science fiction) as "tent-pole" pictures that allow the industry to maintain strong ticket sales even in this age of streaming.

Notwithstanding its story-telling prowess and technical achievement, Ledger's Joker is *TDK*'s obvious attraction; his 44 minutes on screen are mesmerizing and terrifying. Joker is, after all, an "agent of chaos" who brings both Gotham's civic institutions and its "dark guardian" to their respective knees with just "a few drums of gas and a couple of bullets."

No ordinary man, Joker is, instead, a shape-shifting, subversive dynamo – a prototypical "bad clown," uncontained by flesh and blood, who lives "in our imaginations as [a] vigilante antihero … of the id" (Radford, 2016, p. 4). Indeed, the sheer number of classic subversive American personas that Joker inhabits in *TDK* is dizzying. He is: a primitive, bloodthirsty Indian who wears "war paint"; a billionaire robber baron who cares so little for his ill-gotten spoils that he sets aflame a literal mountain of cash; a sexually ambiguous dandy who wears garish designer suits; a serial killer who disfigures his victims with knives, savoring the terrified "little emotions" that they express before the fatal act; a suicidal nihilist who implores Batman to run him down at high speed; a confidence man whose compulsive lies about both his origins and his criminal schemes are designed to elicit desire in his marks; a reality television prodigy whose grotesque command of the airwaves is impossible to ignore; a corrupt cop who attempts to assassinate Gotham's mayor; and a cross-dressing sexy nurse who seduces Gotham's paragon of virtue – its "white knight" – into acts of mass homicide. Lacking an essential identity, his pockets stuffed full only of "knives and lint," Joker is an empty signifier; he is a subversive container for Batman's countersubversive fears and illicit desires.

And Batman's darkest desire, it turns out, is to rain down savage vengeance on both the criminals responsible for his primal trauma *and* the "civilized" people and their institutions of law and order that failed to protect young Bruce Wayne from the savagery that produced that trauma. It is, thus, in an ironic turn also suggested by Morrison's Batman of Zur-en-Arrh, not Batman who "completes" Joker but exactly the opposite. Joker's scheme in *TDK*, to bring down Gotham, is a love letter to the forever traumatized little boy who sought to protect himself from additional blows by dressing up like a bat and scaring the living daylights out of his fellow citizens.

Don't talk like one of them. You're not, even if you'd like to be.

Joker, *The Dark Knight*

Joker schemes to bring righteous vengeance to Gotham law and order, and so also to the "civilized" lives that its institutions and formal actors protect from the savage forces of chaos and disorder. In so doing, he exposes the modern pretense at the heart of Gotham law and order – that "law is reason unaffected by desire" – as nothing more than a "bad joke, dropped at the first sign of trouble." By excavating Gotham's savage, repressed heart, Joker illuminates also the regime of exterminatory, devouring violence that is concealed within the city's countersubversive desire for order. Thus does Joker's scheme point to the truth of Robert Cover's insight that "between the idea and the reality of common meaning falls the shadow of the violence of the law, itself" (Cover, 1986, p. 1630).

Joker realizes immediately that the countersubversive neurosis at the heart of Gotham law and order is most apparent in the city's unofficial partnership with Batman. The practitioners of Gotham law and order invest their own countersubversive desires for savage vengeance in Batman – a vigilante unbound by legal niceties who, as Bruce Wayne's butler Alfred puts it, "can make the choice that no one else can make – the right choice." Indeed, *TDK* shows Batman flouting all manner of legal procedure: he tortures criminal suspects (he drops a mob boss off a second story balcony and beats Joker with his bare hands – in a Gotham City Police Department [GCPD] interrogation room no less); he ignores an extradition treaty by kidnapping a mob associate from his home in Hong Kong and delivering him to Gotham authorities; and he engages in wholesale violation of privacy rights by hacking the cell phones of nearly all of Gotham's residents. None of these actions make Batman a target of Gotham authorities; he is instead a valued resource both for the GCPD and for the city's new District Attorney, its "white knight" Harvey Dent.[24] Thus it is that at the outset of *TDK*, Batman, Captain (later Commissioner) James Gordon, and Dent ally, combining both the reason and desire at law's countersubversive heart, to wage war both on the Gotham mob and the official corruption on which the mob relies.

Joker desires the same things. He is also intent on destroying organized crime in Gotham and rooting out the official corruption that feeds it. But Joker is unbound; he refuses to delude himself into believing that the righteous violence with which he will cleanse Gotham ("everything burns," he affirms) is somehow serving the cause of Gotham "law and order" or the ideals of civilization that law and order venerates. Instead, his scheme is about "sending a message" that Gotham civilization is a façade, a hypocritical veneer of respectability erected and maintained by people who lack the courage to acknowledge the brutality and illicit desire that lurks at the dark heart of Gotham law and order. Shockingly, it turns out that Bruce Wayne secretly agrees with Joker.

But it's more than just intellectual harmony. Joker's every action in *TDK* points to, and realizes, Bruce Wayne's darkest fantasies – the ones that are unsatisfied even when Bruce dons Batman's cape and cowl. Two of these fantasies in particular orient the action in *TDK*. First, audiences learned in Nolan's earlier (2006) *Batman Begins* (BB) that Bruce Wayne holds both Gotham organized crime *and* the corrupt civic institutions and figures who were in league with Gotham mobsters responsible for the murder of his parents; for it was the civic corruption that the mob fostered that depleted Gotham's resources and plunged the city into economic hard times – hard times that produced the types of desperate criminals like the one who murdered Thomas and Martha Wayne in an armed robbery gone wrong (Nolan, 2005). Second, and as audiences also learned in *BB*, Bruce harbors romantic love for his childhood friend Rachel Dawes, who pledges that she will hold a flame for him until he finishes being Batman. Rachel thus represents the potential for a reconstructed family life; future consummation of their romance points to the fulfillment of Bruce's dreams for the "normal life" of which he was deprived by the murder of his parents. Destroy the mob and cleanse Gotham of corruption, on the one hand; succeed in that mission and make a new family with Rachel, on the other hand: the fulfillment of Bruce's deepest desires amount to the healing of his primal trauma.

But at the start of *TDK,* it is clear that things are not going to plan. Batman's war on the Gotham mob has produced major victories and placed the city's organized crime families on the defensive; but it has also, ironically, strengthened those families, who have responded by allying with each other and expanding their reach outside of Gotham (affiliating with, and laundering their money through, a major international conglomerate). Nor has Batman succeeded in purging Gotham's institutions of law and order of corruption; even the virtuous Captain Gordon, who has been placed in charge of a new task force (the Major Crimes Unit), is forced to work with cops who were under investigation at Internal Affairs. The one apparently positive development, the election of a new District Attorney (Harvey Dent) who shares Batman's zeal for destroying the mob and exposing corruption, also complicates Bruce's plans: Dent and Rachel, his Assistant DA, have fallen in love. This latter development leads Bruce to eagerly ally with Dent, in the hopes that if Gotham is purged of crime and corruption and he gives up being Batman, Rachel will leave Dent and marry him. Rachel implies that this will not happen ("Don't make me your one shot at a normal life," she tells him); but Bruce doesn't hear her.

Joker thus enters a Gotham barely changed by Batman's savage war against crime and corruption. The problem, Joker avers, is Batman's "misplaced sense of self-righteousness" – his stubborn insistence on clinging to the porous, fictional boundaries between civilization and savagery, between reason and desire, that constitutes Gotham's countersubversive regime of law and order. Batman, Joker divines, is deluding himself. For deep down, Bruce, "no matter how much [he] wants to," simply does not believe that Gotham's existing order is redeemable from the crime and corruption that defines it. Nor, at bottom, does he believe that he can ever heal from the primal trauma of his parents' murder; the promise of a "normal life" with Rachel is a false dawn, even if she were to leave Dent and take up with him, which he secretly doubts she will do. Joker thus understands that Batman is clinging to unrealizable dreams – dreams that are holding him back from living in a "sensible way."[25]

And so Joker's scheme systematically does what Bruce cannot bring Batman to do: it unleashes a cleansing violence that enacts savage vengeance on Gotham's "civilized," but deeply corrupt people and the institutions of law and order that have protected them, even as innocent people (orphaned children, like Bruce Wayne) have suffered the consequences of this corruption. Joker: infiltrates the Gotham mob with a promise to "kill the Batman" but, once there, murders its leaders, steals its riches, and commandeers its foot soldiers for his own gang; poisons the corrupt police commissioner, murders a corrupt judge, attempts to assassinate Gotham's sleazy mayor, and blows up Gordon's special unit, which is full of corrupt cops (notably, Joker never threatens the noble James Gordon himself); terrorizes Gotham's "trust fund brigade" at a political fundraiser and creates a scenario in which hundreds of Gotham's most privileged citizens reveal their willingness to commit mass homicide to save themselves; murders two more corrupt cops whose names can be combined to spell out "Harvey Dent" and, once realizing that Dent is not the "white knight" he has been made out to be, transforms Dent into the iconic Gotham villain "Two Face" and frees him to commit a series of brutal murders – thus, bringing "him down to our level," Joker tells Batman. And, finally, Joker carries out Bruce's most illicit and disturbing fantasy: he channels Bruce's rage at Rachel over her rejection of him and murders her.

Accordingly, when Joker tells Batman that "you complete me" he is ironically inviting Batman to consider the obverse: that Joker has done nothing more than bring about Bruce Wayne's darkest fantasies and thereby freed him to live a "sensible" life free of the "self-righteousness" and "rules" that have kept him locked in the disturbed, paranoid–schizoid phase of compulsive splitting, repression, and projection. Alfred has already intimated as much to Bruce. Indeed, the butler's diagnosis of Joker as a man who "can't be bought, bullied, reasoned, or negotiated with" and whose deepest desire is to "watch the world burn" applies also to Bruce himself, as the camera's panning back and forth between the faces of Bruce and Joker during Alfred's monologue makes clear.

In their symbiotic, twinned relationship with Joker, both Morrison's Batman of Zur-en-Arrh and Nolan's Dark Knight are portrayed ambivalently: avatars of Gotham law and order, both Batmen guard, but also undermine, Gotham authority. In particular, both portrayals emphasize how Gotham is a din of official corruption that relies upon violent, extralegal suppression (both in the form of conventional law enforcement and condoned vigilante justice) to maintain unearned privilege. Led by a countersubversive regime that is at once exposed, and justified, by the presence of a demonized subversive who is a container for its own illicit desires and exterminatory fantasies, Gotham is a "bad joke" in need of cleansing fire – a fire that it eventually does experience both in Morrison's and Nolan's final Batman storylines.[26] Simultaneously Gotham's dark guardian and its ironic arsonist,[27] Batman's countersubversive heroism exposes how the mythology of modern law that animates Gotham is an unstable, disturbed worldview that relies upon repressing rather than overcoming the "wild beasts" of human desire that constitute it.

4. CONCLUSION

Superhero stories have saturated America's popular culture over the previous 15 years. Scholarly analyses of these stories, including by law and society scholars, have proceeded in step. As we have seen, such analyses have tended to focus on how superheroes point to the weakness of legal procedures and institutions in the face of existential threat. Superheroes are, therefore, analyzed as Bainbridge analyzes them in this "postmodern" era of storytelling: audiences, he argues, are conditioned to view superheroes as necessary complements to a state power that is constrained by increasingly anachronistic legal values, such as respect for due process and the rights of the accused.[28] The goals of substantive justice and righteous vengeance that motivate superheroes in the postmodern age are, thus, imagined as being in opposition to law's modern values of rationality, universality, and consideration (Bainbridge, 2007).[29]

But my analysis here of Grant Morrison and Christopher Nolan's Batman stories complicates matters. In these stories, Batman does not supplement a hyper-rational and procedure-obsessed law – one that fails to achieve the goals of substantive justice and vengeance because such desires apparently fall outside of law's orbit. Batman is instead an essential, if ambivalent, force for law's realization of *exactly those desires* according to hyper-rational, procedural means (he is, after all, a master detective). Batman is in these stories a countersubversive avatar of Gotham law and order; just as modern law represses the "wild beasts" that nevertheless constitute its claims to reason, so does Batman repress his forbidden desires for vengeance and project them onto his dark twin Joker. Then, in prototypical American countersubversive fashion, Batman indulges in the exact destructive, exterminatory fantasies, and behaviors that are ostensibly the exclusive property of the subversive Joker. Batman, indeed, personifies modern law's fantasy of being "reason unaffected by desire," its fantasy of somehow being immune to the repressed desires and hatreds that constitute its *raison d'être*.

Such desires and hatreds, and the countersubversive employments of "rational" legal procedures and institutions to entrench them in governing practices, are hallmarks of modern times (Darian-Smith, 2010; Fitzpatrick, 1992). But tethering modern law's illicit desires to its reason is bound to provoke anxiety (Mezey, 2011). For if modern law is not, in fact, a "big, beautiful wall" that protects us from, for example, the countersubversive fantasies of would-be authoritarians but is instead a repressed instantiation of just those fantasies …

It is unsurprising that many Americans – including, most notably, the current American president – register this anxiety about law. Indeed, Donald Trump, like all prominent American countersubversives, has an extensive history of demonizing the exact behaviors in which he himself engages. He has, for example, lived a life of legally dubious professional and personal behavior and yet he proclaims himself a champion of law and order (Fahrenthold, Zapotosky, & Kim, 2018; Relman, 2019). So too does he rail against the illegal, "alien" invasions of undocumented migrants and the process of "chain migration" with which they reunite with their families in the Unites States, even as his own immigrant First Lady failed to comply with the requirements of her work visa, has evaded questions about how she secured permanent residence status, and who, in 2018, employed the very process that her husband vilifies to attain citizenship status for her parents (Blake, 2018; Correal & Cochrane, 2018; Keneally, 2018).

Thus, does Donald Trump personify the anxiety provoked by modern law's countersubversive pretentions to being "reason unaffected by desire." And, as did Grant Morrison and Christopher Nolan before him, it is an anxiety that Trump translates into a very particular domain of American popular culture. Responding to the query of a 9-year-old boy at a 2015 campaign stop in Iowa, America's future 45th president left no doubt about his countersubversive bona fides: "I am," Trump claimed, "Batman" (Cavna, 2015).

NOTES

1. A bulwark of and for reason, law thwarts the beastly instincts of human rule; "for desire is a wild beast, and passion perverts the minds of rulers, even when they are the best of men" (Aristotle, 1996, p. 88).

2. But as Moustafa's comprehensive 2014 analysis of scholarship on law and authoritarianism reveals, law is employed to entrench authoritarian prerogatives as often as it is used to resist them. This ambiguity, he suggests and I argue here, exists also in putatively democratic nations, such as the United States (Moustafa, 2014, pp. 293–295).

3. On modern law's pretentions to secular rationality, see Eve Darian-Smith's lucid discussion of the "secularization thesis" (Darian-Smith, 2010, pp. 10–13; see also, generally, Sarat, Douglas, & Merrill Umphry, 2006).

4. Foregrounding its repressive force allows us to see, as Ewick (2013) does, how law does not "simply [cover] ... passions, interests, and biases" but how instead its "real power [is] that [it is] implicated in the constitution of these aspects of human 'nature.'" Precisely because it deals in repression, law helps to "produce the unruly, partisan subjects [it is] designed to manage" (Ewick, 2013, p. 200).

5. I am, to be clear, contrasting "authoritarian" to "democratic" practices. Democratic practices, according to the critical tradition of democratic theory to which I am indebted, point to contest, participatory engagement, and the generative possibilities of flourishing dissent and disagreement (see e.g. Honig, 1993; Laclau & Mouffe, 1985). Authoritarian practices, on the other hand, gesture to state attempts to obliterate difference of all sorts, no matter whether those differences are coded as intellectual, racial, gender, sexual, or religious. America's exterminatory countersubversive politics, and their instantiation within our contemporary politics of law and order, are, thus, quintessentially authoritarian in character and impulse (see also Cover, 1983).

6. Manderson's penetrating 2011 essay is representative (Manderson, 2011, pp. 33–35).

7. See also Slotkin ([1973] (2000)) and Morrison (1992).

8. Kristeva refers to the depressive position as the condition of "melancholia" (Kristeva, 1989, generally).

9. On Klein's account of reality testing, and its reliance upon unconscious fantasies, see Segal (1973, pp. 11–23). For a thorough investigation of Klein's account of the "object relations" that dominate early childhood experience, see Kristeva (2001, pp. 57–81).

10. "When the child finds himself in the paranoid–schizoid position", notes Kristeva (2001), "he is afraid that he will be destroyed by the very bad objects that he has projected outside him" (p. 76).

11. "The need to draw rigid boundaries between the alien and the self," affirms Rogin (1987), "suggests fears of too dangerous an intimacy between them" (p. 50). Or, as Kristeva (1996) puts it, "The other is in me. It is my unconscious" (p. 41).

12. "The alien comes to birth as the American's dark double, the imaginary twin who sustains his (or her) brother's identity. Taken inside, the subversive would obliterate the American; driven outside, the subversive becomes an alien who serves as repository for the disowned, negative American self. The alien preserves American identity against fears of boundary collapse and thereby allows the countersubversive, now split from the subversive, to mirror his foe" (Rogin, 1987, p. 284).

13. De León's (2015) extraordinary book documents how American border policy explicitly relies upon harsh desert conditions and predatory wild animals – which together kill, dismember, and scatter the bodies of perished migrants throughout the Sonoran Desert (pp. 23–37; 62–85).

14. "Crime and punishment," according to Scheingold (1991), " [are] symbols for a variety of insecurities associated with unsettling changes in American life" (p. 21). It is thus unsurprising that contemporary post-9/11 anxieties of boundary collapse and bodily invasion, along with historically febrile concerns over what it means to live in a multicultural society, are compulsively featured in popular culture accounts of American law and order (including those accounts, like the ones that I explore here, that include superheroes). For "the play of crime and punishment," affirm Comaroff and Comaroff (2016), "evokes horror and fascination … [it] haunts our moral imaginary" (pp. xii–xiii).

15. To access this American legal gothic, we turn to the products of popular culture – a move that allows us, as D.H. Lawrence famously claimed, to "pull the democratic and idealistic clothes off American utterance, and see what [we] can of the dusky body … underneath" (Lawrence, [1923] (1951), p. 18; see also Fiedler, 1966; Morrison, 1992).

16. Legal meaning, Cramer (2015) agrees, is recursively generated according to popular "discursive and representational practices," regardless of whether those practices are intentionally legal in character (p. 11; see also Calavita, 2010, pp. 31–35).

17. Such concerns, of course, prompted Herbert Packer's (1968) classic discussion of the "due process" and "crime control" models of criminal procedure.

18. Gavaler, for example, traces superhero stories back to early twentieth century popular celebrations of Ku Klux Klan vigilantism. "The superhero," he argues, "originated from an oppressive, racist impulse in American culture, and the formula codifies an ethics of vigilante extremism" (Gavaler, 2012, p. 192).

19. Unsurprisingly (given their twinned relationship), it is typically Joker who reminds audiences of Batman's emotional instability, such as when he quips in *The Dark Knight* that maybe he and Batman could "share" a padded cell (Nolan, 2008). Similarly, in Grant Morrison's first exploration of the Batman–Joker relationship (in *Arkham Asylum*) Joker reminds the reader that the "madhouse" is where Batman "belongs" and even tenderly bids adieu to his "dearest" Batman at the story's conclusion: "Just don't forget – if it ever gets too tough" outside of the asylum "there's always a place for you here." But Joker isn't telling Batman anything that he doesn't already know. "I'm afraid that the Joker may be right about me," confesses Batman. "Sometimes I … question the rationality of my actions. And I'm afraid that when I walk through those asylum gates … It'll be just like coming home" (Morrison & McKean, 1989).

20. In preparation for his role, Nolan had Ledger consult a variety of comic book portraits of Joker, including, prominently, Morrison's (2007a) then-contemporary portrayal of the character as the lunatic "Clown at Midnight." After his death, the character diary that Ledger kept for *The Dark Knight* was discovered in his belongings: it contained lines copied directly from Morrison's comic (Vineyard, 2008).

21. Morrison made clear Joker's primal relationship with Batman in his affiliated 2010 mini-series *The Return of Bruce Wayne*. Recalling Joker's place at the literal beginning of the Batman universe (in 1940s Batman #1), Morrison places a Joker archetype in each

of the historical Gotham settings – its Stone Age-era caves, its seventeenth century Puritan settlements, its eighteenth century pirate coves, its nineteenth century Wild West-like streets and gambling houses, and its 1940s, hard-boiled noir atmospherics – that a time-traveling, amnesiac Bruce Wayne must navigate in order to overcome the effects of Darkseid's Omega Beam and return safely to contemporary Gotham. Joker's pride of place in each era suggests that Morrison's "first truth" of Batman – that Bruce Wayne, in spite of his early orphanage, was never alone – points not to the presence of Bruce's faithful butler Alfred Pennyworth but rather to the constant company of his embedded rage, unfulfilled desires for vengeance, and unremitting guilt over the death of his parents – all of which are revealed in Batman's obsession with his repressed dark twin, Joker (Morrison, 2011a; see also Rollin, 1994, pp. 9–10).

22. It is worth noting, though, that in *Batman Incorporated* #5 (which is a part of Morrison's final Batman storyline), Morrison depicts a presumably imagined future (after Bruce Wayne has died) in which Damian Wayne (Bruce's son) has become the new Batman. In this alternate reality, Dr Simon Hurt is shown as being responsible for Bruce Wayne's death. Now acting as a Machiavellian advisor to the American president, Hurt manipulates POTUS into destroying Gotham with nuclear weapons in an attempt to prevent the spread of a pandemic that is linked to a virulent strain of Joker venom. Morrison makes clear, though, that this is just one possible scenario that a still very-much alive Bruce Wayne has imagined (Morrison, 2013a).

23. In its depiction of Joker as an alternately smitten paramour and jealous lover, 2017's *The Lego Batman Movie* plays the dynamic for laughs (McKay, 2017). This presentation of Batman and Joker's symbiotic relationship through homoerotic terms can be traced back at least as far as Frank Miller's path-breaking 1986 graphic novel *The Dark Knight Returns*. There Miller depicts a catatonic and institutionalized Joker revived at the sight of Batman coming out of his decade-long retirement: "Darling," Joker effuses, as his characteristic grin returns (Miller, 1986).

24. Batman is, for example, given access to crime scenes and evidence, relied upon for forensic expertise, and looked upon as a benefactor who provides Gotham police with law enforcement resources of various sorts.

25. There is no evidence that Joker has figured out that Batman is Bruce Wayne; but he learns of Batman's devotion to Rachel and his disregard for Gotham's "civilized people" early in *TDK*, when Batman leaps through the window of a skyscraper to save Rachel, in the process leaving a penthouse full of Gotham's richest and most powerful people unprotected from Joker and his henchmen. Once Joker figures out that Dent is not Batman, he knows that there is a love triangle at work – but one that simply cannot work out in Batman's favor, for Joker knows that Rachel is devoted to Dent, that she is Dent's "little bunny." Joker, thus, understands that Rachel is simply another encumbrance that is preventing Batman from living the "sensible" life that is the best for which he can hope.

26. Morrison's Batman run ended with *Batman Incorporated*, in which Gotham is destroyed in a battle between Batman and Talia Al-Ghul (Ras's daughter and Batman's former lover, with whom he has a child) (Morrison, 2013b). Nolan's run, meanwhile, ended with *The Dark Knight Rises*, in which Bane (also in league with Talia) systematically demolishes Gotham's civic institutions (including the GCPD) and takes control of the devastated city (Nolan, 2012).

27. I have borrowed the term "ironic arsonist," if not its intent (about which I am [blissfully?] ignorant), from one of my teenaged sons.

28. The contemporary superhero genre is not the only one that imagines legal procedure as, at least at times, an outdated impediment to the realization of justice and security. See, for example, Greenfield's (2001) accounting of "hero lawyers" who systematically ignore established legal procedures and rules (see also Manderson, 2011).

29. An exception to the scholarly common sense is Neal Curtis's illuminating 2016 book, *Sovereigns and Superheroes*. In it, Curtis exposes a "sovereign/beast couplet" at the heart of modern law. This couplet is, I think, consistent with the ambivalent, necessary dynamic between reason and desire that, I have argued here, reveals the countersubversive purpose that propels modern legal practice (Curtis, 2016, p. 69).

ACKNOWLEDGMENTS

I am grateful to the participants of the American Studies Writing Group at the University of Connecticut, who offered helpful comments on an earlier draft. I am also grateful to my UConn Political Science colleagues Stephen Dyson and Fred Lee, each of whom engaged me in multiple conversations about both this specific work and the intersections of law, politics, and popular culture writ large. Anna Kirkland generously provided a close reading of an earlier draft; she productively pushed me to consider an alternative reading of America's contemporary obsession with law and order. I am thankful for the example and support of many law and society scholars (including but not limited to Susan Burgess, Renée Cramer, Austin Sarat, Michael McCann, and William Haltom) who believe, as do I, that the common meanings that circulate in our popular culture are of the utmost importance for understanding the relations between American law, politics, and society. Closer to home, I am grateful to my eldest son Connor, who unwittingly got me interested in the ambivalent meanings of superhero stories when he discovered (and I re-discovered) the *Super Friends* television cartoon when he was 4 years old. My youngest son Andrew, conversely, has enthusiastically attended with me each new blockbuster superhero movie over the preceding years, thus encouraging and contributing to my understanding of the genre. Finally, I am grateful to my spouse Mary, who, in addition to the innumerable ways that she has contributed to the development of my intellectual and scholarly sense over the previous 20 or so years, has kindly refused to ridicule me for the amount of time and energy that I have spent over the last decade thinking about superheroes, and about Batman in particular. Thank you all.

REFERENCES

Alexander, M. (2010). *The new Jim Crow: Mass incarceration in the age of colorblindness*. New York, NY: The New Press.

Aristodemou, M. (2014). *Law, psychoanalysis, society: Taking the unconscious seriously*. New York, NY: Routledge.

Aristotle. (1996). *The politics and the constitution of Athens*. New York, NY: Cambridge University Press.

Bainbridge, J. (2007). 'This is *the Authority*: This planet is under our protection' – An exegesis of superheroes' interrogations of law. *Law, Culture, and the Humanities*, *3*, 455–476.

Bainbridge, J. (2015). 'The call to do justice': Superheroes, sovereigns, and the state during wartime. *International Journal for the Semiotics of Law*, *28*, 745–763.

Blake, A. (2018). The huge questions about Melania Trump's immigration history nobody will answer. *The Washington Post*, February 21. Retrieved from https://www.washingtonpost.com/news/the-fix/wp/2018/02/21/the-huge-questions-about-melania-trumps-immigration-history-nobody-will-answer/

Box Office Mojo. (2008a). 2008 yearly box office results. Retrieved from https://www.boxofficemojo.com/yearly/chart/?yr=2008&p=.htm

Box Office Mojo. (2008b). 2008 yearly box office results. Retrieved from https://www.boxofficemojo.com/alltime/adjusted.htm?sort=gross&order=DESC&adjust_yr=2019&p=.htm

Box Office Mojo. (2009). Academy Awards, 2009. Retrieved from https://www.boxofficemojo.com/oscar/chart/?view=allcategories&yr=2009&p=.htm

Calavita, K. (2010). *Invitation to law and society: An introduction to the study of real law*. Chicago, IL: University of Chicago Press.

Cavna, M. (2015). Donald Trump says he's Batman. Here are 15 reasons why he might just be right. *The Washington Post*, August 18. Retrieved from https://www.washingtonpost.com/news/comic-riffs/wp/2015/08/18/donald-trump-says-hes-batman-here-are-15-reasons-why-he-might-just-be-right/

Comaroff, J., & Comaroff, J. L. (2016). *The truth about crime: Sovereignty, knowledge, social order.* Chicago, IL: University of Chicago Press.

Correal, A., & Cochrane, E. (2018). Melania Trump's parents become U.S. citizens, using 'chain migration' Trump hates. *The New York Times*, August 9. Retrieved from https://www.nytimes.com/2018/08/09/nyregion/melania-trumps-parents-become-us-citizens.html

Cover, R. M. (1975). *Justice accused: Antislavery and the judicial process.* New Haven, CT: Yale University Press.

Cover, R. M. (1983). The Supreme Court, 1982 Term. Foreword: Nomos and narrative. *Harvard Law Review, 97,* 4–68.

Cover, R. M. (1986). Violence and the word. *Yale Law Journal, 95,* 1601–1629.

Cramer, R. A. (2015). *Pregnant with the stars: Watching and wanting the celebrity baby bump.* Stanford, CA: Stanford University Press.

Curtis, N. (2016). *Sovereigns and superheroes.* Manchester: Manchester University Press.

Darian-Smith, E. (2010). *Religion, race, rights: Landmarks in the history of modern Anglo-American Law.* Portland, OR: Hart Publishing.

De León, J. (2015). *The land of open graves: Living and dying on the migrant trail.* Berkeley, CA: University of California Press.

Dudas, J. R. (2017). *Raised right: Fatherhood in modern American conservatism.* Stanford, CA: Stanford University Press.

Ewick, P. (2013). Principles, passions, and the paradox of modern law: A comment on Bybee. *Law and Social Inquiry, 38*(1), 196–205.

Fahrenthold, D. A., Zapotosky, M., & Kim, S. M. (2018). Mounting legal threats surround trump as nearly every organization he has led is under investigation. *The Washington Post*, December 15. Retrieved from https://www.washingtonpost.com/politics/mounting-legal-threats-surround-trump-as-nearly-every-organization-he-has-led-is-under-investigation/2018/12/15/4cfb4482-ffbb-11e8-862a-b6a6f3ce8199_story.html

Fiedler, L. (1966). *Love and death in the American novel.* New York, NY: Delta/Dell Publishing.

Fitzpatrick, P. (1992). *The mythology of modern law.* New York, NY: Routledge.

Gavaler, C. (2012). The Ku Klux Klan and the birth of the superhero. *Journal of Graphic Novels and Comics, 2,* 191–208.

Giddens, T. (2015). Natural law and vengeance: Jurisprudence on the streets of Gotham. *International Journal for the Semiotics of Law, 4,* 765–785.

Goodrich, P. (1995). Maladies of the legal soul: Psychoanalysis and interpretation in law. *Washington & Lee Law Review, 54,* 1035–1074.

Gottschalk, M. (2015). *Caught: The prison state and the lockdown of American politics.* Princeton, NJ: Princeton University Press.

Greenfield, S. (2001). Hero or villain? Cinematic lawyers and the delivery of justice. *Journal of Law and Society, 28,* 25–39.

Hall, S. (1997). Subjects in history: Making diasporic identities. In W. Lubiano (Ed.), *The house that race built: Original essays by Toni Morrison, Angela Y. Davis, Cornel West and others on Black Americans and politics in America today* (pp. 289–299). New York, NY: Pantheon Books.

Haltom, W., & McCann, W. M. (2004). *Distorting the law: Politics, media, and the litigation crisis.* Chicago, IL: University of Chicago Press.

Honig, B. (1993). *Political theory and the displacement of politics.* Ithaca, NY: Cornell University Press.

Jordan, W. D. (1968). *White over black: American attitudes toward the Negro, 1550–1812.* Chapel Hill, NC: University of North Carolina Press.

Keneally, M. (2018). 8 times Trump slammed 'chain migration' before it apparently helped wife's parents become citizens. *ABC News*, August 10. Retrieved from https://abcnews.go.com/US/times-trump-slammed-chain-migration-apparently-helped-wifes/story?id=57132429

Khan, M., Sands, G., &Turner, T. (2018). Trump administration wants $18B to build 'big, beautiful wall.' *ABC News*, January 5. Retrieved from https://abcnews.go.com/Politics/trump-administration-18b-build-big-beautiful-wall/story?id=52172319

Klein, M. (1975). Love, guilt, and reparation. In M. Klein (Ed.), *Love, guilt, and reparation and other works 1921–1945* (pp. 306–343). New York, NY: The Free Press.

Klein, M. (1986). The psycho-analytic play technique. In J. Mitchell (Ed.), *The selected Melanie Klein* (pp. 35–54). New York, NY: The Free Press.

Korte, G., & Gomez, A. (2018). Trump ramps up rhetoric on undocumented immigrants: 'These aren't people. These are animals.' *USA Today*, May 16.

Kristeva, J. (1989). *Black sun: Depression and melancholia*. L. S. Roudiez (Trans.). New York, NY: Columbia University Press.

Kristeva, J. (1996). Cultural strangeness and the subject in crisis. In R. M. Guberman (Ed.), *Julia Kristeva interviews* (pp. 35–60). New York, NY: Columbia University Press.

Kristeva, J. (2001). *Melanie Klein*. R. Guberman (Trans.). New York, NY: Columbia University Press.

Laclau, E., & Mouffe, C. (1985). *Hegemony and socialist strategy*. New York, NY: Verso.

Lawrence, D. H. [1923] (1951). *Studies in classic American literature*. Garden City, NY: Doubleday & Company, Inc.

Lee, F. (2018). *Extraordinary racial politics: Four events in the constitution of the United States*. Philadelphia, PA: Temple University Press.

Longazel, J. (2016). *Undocumented fears: Immigration and the politics of divide and conquer in Hazleton, Pennsylvania*. Philadelphia, PA: Temple University Press.

Manderson, D. (2011). Trust us justice: *24*, popular culture, and the law. In A. Sarat (Ed.), *Imagining legality: Where law meets popular culture* (pp. 22–52). Tuscaloosa, AL: University of Alabama Press.

McCann, M. W., & Haltom, W. (2008). Nothing to believe in: Lawyers in contemporary films about public interest litigation. In A. Sarat & S. Scheingold (Eds.), *The cultural lives of cause lawyers* (pp. 230–252). New York, NY: Cambridge University Press.

McKay, C. (Dir.). (2017). *The Lego Batman Movie*. DC Entertainment.

Mezey, N. (2011). Law's visual afterlife: Violence, popular culture, and translation theory. In A. Sarat (Ed.), *Imagining legality: Where law meets popular culture* (pp. 65–99). Tuscaloosa, AL: University of Alabama Press.

Miller, F. (1986). *The dark knight returns*. New York, NY: DC Comics.

Morrison, G. (2007a). *Batman #663: The clown at midnight*. New York, NY: DC Comics.

Morrison, G. (2007b). *Batman and son*. New York, NY: DC Comics.

Morrison, G. (2008a). Last rites. In G. Morrison (Ed.), *Batman R.I.P.: The Deluxe edition* (pp. 165–216). New York, NY: DC Comics.

Morrison, G. (2008b). *Batman: The black glove*. New York, NY: DC Comics.

Morrison, G. (2009). *Batman R.I.P.: The Deluxe edition*. New York, NY: DC Comics.

Morrison, G. (2011a). *Batman: The return of Bruce Wayne, Deluxe edition*. New York, NY: DC Comics.

Morrison, G. (2011b). *Batman and Robin: Batman and Robin must die! The Deluxe edition*. New York, NY: DC Comics.

Morrison, G. (2013a). *Batman incorporated #5: Asylum*. New York, NY: DC Comics.

Morrison, G. (2013b). *Batman incorporated, Volume 2*. New York, NY: DC Comics.

Morrison, G., & McKean, D. (1989). *Batman: Arkham Asylum – A serious house on serious earth*. New York, NY: DC Comics.

Morrison, T. (1992). *Playing in the dark: Whiteness and the literary imagination*. New York, NY: Vintage Books.

Moustafa, T. (2014). Law and courts in authoritarian regimes. *Annual Review of Law and Social Science*, *10*, 281–299.

Nielsen, L. B., Patel, N. A., & Rosner, J. (2013). 'Ahead of the Lawmen': Law and morality in Disney animated films 1960–1998. *Law, Culture, and the Humanities*, *13*, 104–122.

Nolan, C. (Dir.). (2005). *Batman begins*. Warner Brothers.

Nolan, C. (Dir.). (2008). *The dark knight*. Warner Brothers.

Nolan, C. (Dir.). (2012). *The dark knight rises*. Warner Brothers.

Packer, H. L. (1968). *The limits of the criminal sanction*. Stanford, CA: Stanford University Press.

Peaslee, R. M., & Weiner, R. G. (Eds.). (2015). *The joker: A serious study of the clown prince of crime*. Jackson, MI: University of Mississippi Press.

Phippen, J. W. (2017). What Trump doesn't understand about MS-13. *The Atlantic*, June 26.

Radford, B. (2016). *Bad clowns*. Albuquerque, NM: University of New Mexico Press.

Relman, E. (2019). The 23 women who have accused Trump of sexual misconduct. *Business Insider*, February 25.

Rogin, M. P. (1987). *Ronald Reagan, the movie: And other episodes in political demonology*. Berkeley, CA: University of California Press.

Rogin, M. P. [1975] (1991). *Fathers and children: Andrew Jackson and the subjugation of the American Indian*. New York, NY: Transaction Publishers.

Rollin, L. (1994). Guilt and the unconscious in *Arkham Asylum*. *Inks: Cartoon and Comic Art Studies, 1*, 2–13.

Rotten Tomatoes. (2008). Top 100 movies of 2008. Retrieved from https://www.rottentomatoes.com/top/bestofrt/?year=2008

Sarat, A. (2011). What popular culture does for, and to, law: An introduction. In A. Sarat (Ed.), *Imagining legality: Where law meets popular culture* (pp. 1–21). Tuscaloosa, AL: University of Alabama Press.

Sarat, A., Douglas, L., & Merrill Umphry, M. (Eds.). (2006). *Law and the sacred*. Stanford, CA: Stanford University Press.

Sarat, A., & Scheingold, S. (2008). Bringing cultural analysis to the study of cause lawyers: An introduction. In A. Sarat & S. Scheingold (Eds.), *The cultural lives of cause lawyers* (pp. 1–24). New York, NY: Cambridge University Press.

Scheingold, S. A. (1991). *The politics of street crime: Criminal process and popular obsession*. Philadelphia, PA: Temple University Press.

Segal, H. (1973). *Introduction to the work of Melanie Klein* (New, Enlarged Edition). New York, NY: Basic Books.

Slotkin, R. [1973] (2000). *Regeneration through violence: The mythology of the American frontier, 1600–1860*. Norman, OK: University of Oklahoma Press.

Slotkin, R. [1985] (1998). *The fatal environment: The myth of the frontier in the age of industrialization, 1800–1890*. Norman, OK: University of Oklahoma Press.

Smith, N. R. (2019). *Contradictions of democracy: Vigilantism and rights in post-apartheid South Africa*. New York, NY: Oxford University Press.

Starlin, J., Aparo, J., & DeCarlo, M. (1988). *Batman: A death in the family*. New York, NY: DC Comics.

The Ringer. (2018). The 50 best superhero movies of all time. Retrieved from http://superheroes.theringer.com/

Turesky, J. (2018). Fox News says migrant caravan will bring disease, It won't. *WGBH: Boston Public Radio*, October 31.

Vineyard, J. (2008). 'Arkham asylum' scribe Grant Morrison opens up Heath Ledger's Joker diary. *MTV News*, August 4.

Weldon, G. (2016). *The caped crusade: Batman and the rise of nerd culture*. New York, NY: Simon & Schuster.

CHAPTER 4

THE ROLE OF SOCIAL MEDIA COMPANIES IN THE REGULATION OF ONLINE HATE SPEECH

Chara Bakalis and Julia Hornle

ABSTRACT

This chapter is about online hate speech propagated via platforms operated by social media companies (SMCs). It examines the options open to states in forcing SMCs to take responsibility for the hateful content that appears on their sites. It examines the technological and legal context for imposing legal obligations on SMCs, and analyses initiatives in Germany, the United Kingdom, the European Union and elsewhere. It argues that while SMCs can play a role in controlling online hate speech, there are limitations to what they can achieve.

Keywords: Hate speech; hate crime; Internet regulation; social media regulation; online hate speech; cyberhate

1. INTRODUCTION

This chapter is about online hate propagated via platforms operated by social media companies (SMCs), and it examines the options open to states in forcing SMCs to take responsibility for the hateful content that appears on their sites. The focus will be on the United States and Europe. The chapter explains the dilemma we face if SMCs are to be held responsible for user-generated content, particularly with respect to balancing freedom of expression with the need to offer protection from hate speech. However, this dilemma is not examined through a human rights

Studies in Law, Politics, and Society, Volume 85, 75–100
ISSN: 1059-4337/doi:10.1108/S1059-433720210000085005

law analysis by balancing specific freedom of expression restrictions with harms. Instead, we examine the legal obligations and responsibilities imposed on SMCs as Internet intermediaries in the wake of recent legislative initiatives in some EU Member States. In particular, we chart how the approach has changed from specific notice and take-down obligations to greater responsibilities of proactive measures. We contrast this "European" approach with the US approach under the first Amendment which would prohibit the imposition of such responsibilities.

This chapter argues that regulation in Europe is moving away from giving SMCs as Internet intermediaries immunity from liability for illegal hate speech towards a new approach forcing them to take responsibility for user-generated content, and imposing a range of obligations on them to proactively moderate and manage content on their sites. Furthermore, we argue that as a matter of principle, this approach can be made compliant with freedom of expression obligations under the European Convention on Human Rights (ECHR) in a way that might not be possible under freedom of speech rules under the US First Amendment. However, we point to the concern that some of the pro-active measures, to the extent that they automate content moderation and management, do create particular concerns over freedom of expression, and, therefore, require particular attention.

The growth of online hate has been exponential over the last few years (O'Regan, 2018). Although we do not have official statistics that can give us an accurate picture of the actual amount of online hate, several recent studies have found alarming levels of abuse. For example, the Anti-Defamation League (2019) found that 37% of Americans had suffered online harassment, and that a third of these cases were as a result of the target's protected characteristic such are race, religion, gender identity, sexual orientation or disability. A report by Amnesty International (2019) found that an abusive or problematic tweet was sent to a female politician every 30 seconds and that black women were 84% more likely than white women to receive abusive tweets. Meanwhile, a Canadian survey found that 60% of Canadians had viewed hate speech online (Association for Canadian Studies, 2019).

There are a number of factors, however, that make the regulation of online hate particularly difficult (Bakalis, 2017; O'Regan, 2018). For example, the sheer scale of the amount of online hate, the pseudonymity afforded by the Internet, and jurisdictional issues when the perpetrators of hate and their victims do not live in the same country make this a very difficult area to police. Particularly controversial is the issue of free speech which creates difficulties in introducing legislation to prohibit this sort of material. In spite of these difficulties, governments across the world are coming under increasing pressure to do something about the problem, particularly as it is becoming progressively more obvious that this is a particular problem for minority groups.

More recently, the focus has shifted onto social media providers and their responsibility for contributing to the dissemination of online hate speech (Cohen-Almagor, 2015; Laidlaw, 2015). Politicians and social activists have called on SMCs to "do more" to prevent the spread of hate speech, abuse and extremist content on their platforms. While the discussion in the early 2000s mainly focused on the question of technological innovation and immunity for intermediaries, and a narrow tailored notice and take-down obligation, recently the debate has called for greater SMC responsibility, and concomitant with this, pro-active and much more extensive obligations to manage and monitor content (Frosio, 2018).

The focus on SMCs has come about because of the growing realization that policing online hate by law enforcers is virtually impossible because of the sheer amount of hate that appears online, and the recognition that SMCs are, therefore, much better placed to deal with this because they have a degree of technical control over their platforms.

However, placing the responsibility on social media providers brings with it its own problems, and is not necessarily the quick, easy and cheap solution that politicians may hope for, particularly, in relation to any proposal which aims to automate the process of removing hateful material.

Currently, in the United States and Europe, SMCs are operating in a sphere that was predicated on the ideals of freedom from governmental regulation and laws. Since the early days of the Internet and the World Wide Web, there was an acknowledgment that platform providers cannot be treated akin to offline publishers of the information they allowed to appear on their platforms, as they lack control over the content itself (Bridy, 2018; Murray, 2016). The Communications Decency Act 1996 (CDA) was enacted in the United States to give protection to service providers from being treated as publishers or distributers of the content they hosted. This was followed in 2000 at the EU level by the E-Commerce Directive 2000//31/EC. While the CDA gives absolute immunity to publishers (other than immunity from Federal criminal law), Article 14 of the E-commerce Directive bases immunity for hosting providers on a knowledge standard. Thus, SMCs are shielded from liability only if they do not know (e.g. through notification or constructive knowledge) that they are hosting illegal content. However, the E-Commerce Directive states that no general obligation can be imposed on SMCs to monitor their platforms.

In this context, the main way in which the pressure on SMCs has manifested itself has been in the form of voluntary codes of conduct such as that set up by the Working Group on Cyberhate convened by the Anti-Defamation League in the United States, and the EU Voluntary Code of Conduct (2016). However, in the last 2 years, political pressure has been growing and SMCs have been called upon to "do more." Consequently, we have seen legislative initiatives moving in two directions: one type of legislation imposes standards for the speed and quality of notice and take-down, and the second type of initiatives have moved from mere take-down obligations to imposing a range of pro-active measures.

Thus, in Europe, the tide appears to be turning, and governments are actively rethinking regulation. For example, in Germany, politicians were impatient with the apparent lack of action by SMCs in taking down content that is illegal according to German law. As a consequence, the Network Law Enforcement Act[1] was enacted in 2017 which seeks to impose a legal obligation on Internet platform providers to act swiftly to remove hateful material from the Internet. The French Parliament recently passed similar legislation, although this was ultimately struck down by the Constitutional Court for being incompatible with freedom of expression. Initiatives have also been taken in the United Kingdom and at the EU level where greater responsibility on SMCs is envisaged, and which will be discussed further below.

It will be argued that while there may be a good case for imposing some of the burden for the regulation of cyberhate on platform providers, in reality they are limited in what they can do. We also have to be careful that any law requiring SMCs to remove or block certain types of online speech does not unintentionally confer on them too much power over what can and cannot be said online. Instead, what is needed is a proper discussion about the regulation of cyberhate, an acceptance that SMCs are limited in what they can do, and the acknowledgment that in fact a multi-faceted approach is required.

The first section of this chapter will outline what technological possibilities are open to SMCs to control hateful content. It will be argued that they are better placed to remove online hate than the police, but that there are real limitations on their ability to do this. There are also problems with requiring SMCs to proactively monitor content. In particular, the use of automated content moderation and reliance on private regulatory regimes may mean that perfectly legal content is taken down. The second section will locate the regulatory options within free speech concerns and will argue that the approach adopted by each country needs to reflect the legal norms of each jurisdiction. The final section will look at current developments in a number of European countries and at the EU level and place them in the context of freedom of speech.

To preface this discussion, two definitions need to be made at the outset.

The definition of hate speech is contested but, for the purposes of the argument in this article, it will include content which is illegal under legislation aimed at outlawing speech that incites violence, hatred or discrimination against named groups. We take "hate speech" to refer to a narrow category of material that is illegal under the law, thus, distinguishing it from material that might express hateful content, but which is not in fact illegal. It is also important to distinguish hate speech from general hate crime provisions which, at their most simplistic, can be defined as crimes that deal with behavior that is already recognized as criminal under the law (such as assault), but which are aggravated because of the perceived hostility of the perpetrator against the victim based on their affiliation to a particular group. By contrast, hate speech provisions are ones which criminalize *speech* on the basis of its hateful content against certain groups.

Social media have been defined (Boyd & Ellison, 2007) as

> web-based services that allow individuals to (1) construct a public or semi-public profile within a bounded system, (2) articulate a list of other users with whom they share a connection, and (3) view and transverse their list of connections and those made by others within the system.

We define SMCs for the purpose of this Article as providers of a platform environment which allows users to upload content ("user-generated content") to share and communicate this content with other users (whether they are a restricted group of contacts, everyone registered on the platform, or more generally with users searching content online). This definition includes major providers such as Facebook, Instagram, Snapchat, WhatsApp, Twitter and YouTube, but also smaller providers. We acknowledge that there is a need to define more clearly between, on the one hand, messaging services, whose main purpose is communication among a limited circle of private users, and, on the other hand, content-sharing services whose main purpose is the sharing and distribution of multi-media content which originates with users of the service. We adopt this wide definition not because of a normative argument about the scope of legal regulation, but for the reason that some of the laws and regulations discussed below have such a wide scope, and for the reason that this article canvasses the issues widely. The focus of this chapter is not a classification of different types of services and their functions, although we acknowledge that more research and conceptualization is needed for the regulatory debate.

What defines SMCs is that their users entirely determine the user-generated content, but the SMCs are in control of arranging the content through metadata and online profiling, and they control the methods and format of the users' interaction (e.g. by having a wall with posts or "likes" of content).

2. WHAT *CAN* SMCS DO TO PREVENT ONLINE HATE BEING DISSEMINATED?

To be in a position to evaluate the recent initiatives in the field of online hate and platform liability, it is important first to outline what exactly SMCs *can* do from a technological and logistical point of view to curb the mass of online hate on their sites. By delineating the parameters of what SMCs can do, it will be seen that there are real limitations to, and dangers *inherent* in, the technology available to them that are sometimes ignored by politicians when they demand that SMCs should "do more" to control online hate.

In answering this question, it is crucial at the outset to make a distinction between re-active content moderation and pro-active moderation. With reactive moderation, content is only taken down after a complaint has been made to the SMC of a potential breach of community guidelines or law. This is also known as notice and take-down. Pro-active content moderation is where material is prevented from being posted, and *before* it has been notified by anyone.

2.1. Re-active Notice and Take-down

Notice and Take-down is essentially a reactive form of content moderation whereby SMCs react to notification by users, or organizations they work with, and take content down, or close accounts, groups or channels. Given that SMCs may be liable under the applicable national law unless they take down material expeditiously once they have been notified by their users, a number of SMCs, and in particular the tech giants, have set up notice and take-down systems and procedures.

Facebook has stated publicly that it had 7,500 reviewers in 2018 and had plans to double the members of staff working on safety and security to 20,000 before the end of 2018 (US Senate Committee, 2018). YouTube has been running a "flagging system," whereby content flagged by users is reviewed. In addition, YouTube has developed a "trusted flagger programme" which is a community of trusted users who have a track record of flagging content accurately, according to YouTube's content guidelines (US Senate Committee, 2018). YouTube has described its trusted flaggers as organizations with specialist expertise, for example, in hate speech and terrorism, and that it expanded its trusted flagger programme by an additional 50 NGOs during 2017. It stated that it would have 10,000 persons working to fight content which violates YouTube content guidelines in 2018, and that it removed 70% of violent extremism videos within 8 hours of uploading (US Senate Committee, 2018).

One of the main challenges of notice and take-down is that for some types of content and communications this mechanism is too slow, even if take-down takes place within a few hours of notification. For example, on Twitter conversations develop and escalate quickly, and the impact of the content occurs very soon after the tweet has been published – practically in real time (O'Regan, 2018). Hence, for Twitter, the action it takes on notification is to close accounts, and it stated that until January 2018 it had closed 1.1 million accounts which it had classified as terrorist accounts. However, Twitter also admitted that around 5% of its approximately 300 million accounts are fake accounts, many of which are automated bot accounts (US Senate Committee, 2018), which turns the take-down process into a constant fight against the hydra monster of ancient Greek mythology.

But even assuming that SMCs take down content quickly and according to clear guidelines – say within 1 hour or 24 hours as has been suggested in the EU Proposal for terrorist content or as is the case under the German Network Law Enforcement Act – its negative impact may nevertheless already have been considerable as 1,000s, if not 100,000s of users may have seen the content and it may already have been copied, reposted or retweeted to other corners of the Internet, including smaller SMCs and hosting companies or companies who refuse to take action against illegal content (Commission Staff Working Document, 2018). In particular, certain SMC applications, such as Facebook Live (live streaming of video), have led to irreversible online harm at the instant that the content is published. For example, the filming of the terrible terrorist attack on mosques in Christchurch in New Zealand, which, even though it was taken down within an hour of upload, had already been viewed 4,000 times before it was removed (BBC News (1), 2019). The Prime Minister of New Zealand, Jacinda Ardern, has stated that she wants the Facebook Live facility to be changed, for example, by incorporating a delay before the stream goes live, and she is urging G7 countries to take action to mandate such a restriction (BBC News (2), 2019).

Furthermore, an investigation by the German newspaper, Süddeutsche Zeitung (SZ) back in 2016–2017 revealed how these content moderation systems work in practice: Facebook, for example, receives 46 million take-down requests a week, which means that its 4,000 reviewers have about 8 seconds to make a decision whether to take content down (Süddeutsche Report, 2016). The reviews are outsourced to several service companies across the globe, where the reviewers usually work just above the minimum wage, and after 2 weeks of training have to review around 2,000–3,000 pieces of content a day, some of which is so heinous that it leaves them traumatized with the outsourced service company providing little in terms of psychological support (Guardian News, 2018). Some of the content moderators in their interviews with the SZ admitted that the time pressure and the nature of the materials is such that they have given up looking at the pictures properly. There are, therefore, serious questions to be asked about the protection of the employees of the outsourced services, and also about the quality of the notice and take-down process and decision-making (The Cleaners Documentary, 2018).

Considering how complex and context-specific the assessment is, and considering that editorial decisions require careful deliberation, the take-down process has rightly been criticized even though the major SMCs have employed more staff and are working on improving their processes (US Senate Committee, 2018).

Moreover, there are questions about the transparency of the internal rules and guidelines made by the SMCs. These internal guidelines, according to which moderators take content down, were originally secret, but were leaked by the UK newspaper, the Guardian, in 2017. In 2018, Facebook published its community standards in response to that leak (Guardian News, 2018). Such transparency has also been demanded by the EU Commission's Communication on Tackling Illegal Content Online (EU Commission, 2017). Therefore, while notice and take-down is established as a mechanism, it continues to involve substantial challenges. However, even greater challenges are inherent in pro-active content moderation by SMCs, which we turn to next.

2.2. Pro-active Prevention of Dissemination

The second way in which SMCs can control their user-generated content is through pro-active prevention or dissemination where content is blocked as it is being posted and before it has been notified by anyone. Frequently, technology aids this process and the temptation for politicians is to call for automation through the use of artificial intelligence.

Owing to the sheer quantity of information posted and uploaded by users on social media every second (YouTube famously quoted the hours of videos uploaded every second as being 400 hours) and every day (there are an estimated 5 million tweets every day), it is impossible to monitor content or exercise editorial responsibility on a manual basis. Therefore, the only realistic way in which content can be proactively removed is through the use of artificial intelligence which filters material at super-human speeds and identifies and blocks material that is deemed unacceptable by community standards, or illegal under national laws.

Algorithmic tools used for content filtering are extremely limited in what they can identify as the subject matter of a video, an image or a text, and are by themselves not yet matured to distinguish between lawful and illegal content (Ammar, 2019; UN Special Rapporteur, 2018). An illustration of this is that automated tools have difficulties distinguishing between an image of a medical operation and that of an execution, or to distinguish between different meanings of the same word (think e.g. of the Russian feminist activist band "Pussy Riot"). Furthermore, algorithmic tools currently cannot understand the context of the information before them, and, therefore, find it hard to pick up on parody, satire, irony or jokes. They also cannot recognize the context where a user actively and explicitly criticizes an image or where they have reposted a quote. Because of this, there is a risk that automated tools may lead to the removal of counter-speech aimed at hate or even terrorist speech in a counter-productive way (Frosio, 2018). Since the legality or illegality of speech frequently turns on context, this makes automating the legal assessment extremely challenging, if not impossible. Moreover, for some types of speech, the legal assessment depends on whether the information is factually true or not, so that extraneous information must be sought before a decision can be made. Finally, there is a risk that if content is taken down by automated tools without human review, important evidence of crime or items of news reporting are made unavailable to investigators or security services. Therefore, automated detection of new illegal content and its classification at present requires human verification (Commission Staff Working Document, 2018).

Despite these shortcomings, the large SMCs have invested in automated content recognition and blocking technology, and so have governments, particularly in the context of material relating to terrorism (Wired, 2018).

Facebook has stated that it proactively uses algorithms for text-based machine learning and hashes for matching images which have been previously identified as illegal online extremism (US Senate Committee, 2018). Once a terrorist video or image has been identified as illegal, such known content is taken down within one hour.

It also stated that this automated technology proactively discovers more than 99% of Al Quaeda and IS propaganda material online before it was notified to Facebook (US Senate Committee, 2018). Likewise, YouTube stated that it has invested in machine-learning technologies and uses a classification system which pro-actively flags videos for human review as potentially extremist hate speech, and that this has enabled YouTube to remove nearly five times as many videos. YouTube also uses image-matching techniques which prevent the re-upload of extremist videos (US Senate Committee, 2018). Similar to the figures quoted by Facebook, YouTube stated that 98% of videos taken down were initially identified by algorithms, not notification. Twitter also stated that it has developed technology automating the recognition of terrorist accounts before they are reviewed by a human reviewer, and that in 2017, 90% of terrorist accounts were identified by these automated tools and 75% of these accounts were closed before anything was tweeted from them (US Senate Committee, 2018). The combination of artificial intelligence and human review has increased the quantity of illegal content removed and has sped up the process.

Facebook, YouTube and Twitter have also invested in counter-speech initiatives such as the "Peer-to-Peer Challenging Extremism Programme" and the "Creators for Change Programme." These initiatives address the filter-bubble silo problem whereby website algorithms target content to users based on behavioral online profiling and leads to users being caught in content which is highly selective and isolating (Pariser, 2011). They specifically target content critical of violent extremism and containing counter-narratives to users who seem interested in violent extremism and terrorist content (US Senate Committee, 2018).

However, a number of services exist (such as Telegram) which offer encryption to their users, which means that they cannot deploy automated content monitoring. This makes the pro-active detection of illegal content impossible. Moreover, automated monitoring is challenged by the fact that terrorist organizations and organizations which spread online hate change their tactics and online strategies in such a way that it is more difficult to automatically recognize such content as online hate or terrorist content.

Finally, Facebook, YouTube and Twitter have a shared database of hashes of known terrorist images and videos, which they use to filter uploads, thus, preventing this content to be spread across their platforms. This technology creates a unique hash function or digital fingerprint against which other images and videos can be compared. Digital fingerprinting was first used for this purpose in the context of images of child abuse by the National Center for Missing and Exploited Children which uses a technology called PhotoDNA to find known images of abused children. It has also been used for preventing the dissemination of images or music videos (e.g. YouTube's Content Id) that infringe copyright. Now SMCs are deploying this technology to ensure extremist images and videos (e.g. beheadings or propaganda lectures) are removed and stay down (US Senate Committee, 2018).

Thus, while AI can certainly be of some help in pro-actively identifying and removing illegal hate speech, it is clear that there are real questions over whether and how this kind of proactive content monitoring can be or should be achieved. There are two main arguments against automated, pro-active filtering without human assessment. First, there is the argument that this type of pro-active filtering is ineffective, or even, in some instances, counter-productive (Ammar, 2019). Such filtering may be counter-productive as it would remove content uploaded to steer would-be-terrorists away from extremist content. Second, there is the danger of the removal of material that is legal, and thereby infringing freedom of expression through excessive censorship.

Summing up, it is clear that that there is a huge quantity of heinous content about which users complain, which SMCs have enabled, and which they now find difficult to control. There is a financial burden attached to this, but for the largest SMCs at least, it seems only fair that they plough more of their huge profits into protecting both users and their moderators, and that they share some of the resources with smaller or not-for-profit SMCs.

The call for SMCs to take greater responsibility for policing their platforms has had some success in improving both notice and take-down, and has also led to investment in automated tools which can ensure the stay-down of images and videos, and can pro-actively detect online hate, and in particular terrorist content. This has sped up detection. However, it is equally clear that artificial intelligence tools cannot completely automate detection and prevent the upload of illegal online hate in the foreseeable future, because of the context sensitivity of such materials and changing strategies of groups propagating such materials. While it is equally clear that using such tools may speed up the process of detection and action against known types of content, actual removal nevertheless requires human review in many cases. There is, therefore, still a question mark over whether it is indeed possible to gain control over the sheer overwhelming quantity of hate materials, and the use of sophisticated technology such as bots posting such material, or encryption by groups propagating hate.

Politically it is convenient to call for artificial intelligence, machine learning and other technology to solve the problem, but the danger is indeed that this call brushes under the carpet the real complexity of the issues involved, including undermining freedom of expression and the question to what extent removal of content may have unintended, counter-productive side effects. Therefore, it is important to keep in mind the need to build in safeguards, such as demanding that content automatically detected is reviewed by a human reviewer, and demanding quality standards as to the training and support of such human reviewers.

3. PUTTING THE REGULATORY APPROACHES INTO THE CONTEXT OF INTERNET FREE SPEECH

Having examined the technological capabilities of SMCs, this next section will situate the regulatory approaches into the context of free speech. Regulation of online hate has often been opposed because of concerns about free speech. This section will examine these concerns and will argue that the approach adopted by a state should be guided by its own cultural and legal stance on hate speech as well as by broader questions over Internet regulation. This is an important insight as the debate in this area has largely been driven by US First Amendment considerations. This has distorted and derailed the debate, particularly in European countries which have established hate speech laws that do not align with the United States approach on hate speech. It is crucial that the US-bias in the debate is recognized in order for the discussion in this area to develop and evolve in a way that is more consistent with the cultural and legal norms of each individual country or region.

Until relatively recently, the default position in relation to hate speech has been to avoid enacting any binding legal obligations on SMCs to remove hateful material from their platforms. This default position has been based partly on the concept of "cyberlibertarianism" which is the school of thought that believes that our concepts of traditional state sovereignty do not work in the virtual world, and so regulation of the Internet is impossible and futile (Johnson & Post, 1996). But it is also partly shaped by the US First Amendment view of the issue which does not necessarily fit with the legal norms and culture elsewhere in the world (Beliveau, 2018).

In the United States, freedom of speech is guaranteed under the First Amendment of the Constitution which states that "Congress shall make no law … abridging the freedom of speech …" (First Amendment). Supreme Court jurisprudence has finessed and delineated the parameters of the right to free speech. In relation to hate speech, the Supreme Court has ruled in a number of cases that hate speech is protected free speech, and states can only prohibit speech if it incites "imminent lawless action" (*Brandenburg* v. *Ohio*, 1969). In the case of *R.A.V.* v. *City of St Paul* (1992), the Supreme Court confirmed that any rules which prohibit the content of speech (such as hate speech) are unconstitutional. It still remains possible, for states to prohibit speech if it constitutes "fighting words" and, thus, incites violence. It is, however, unconstitutional for states to create laws that prohibit any speech based purely on its hateful content.

In addition to this, the Supreme Court in *ACLU* v. *Reno* (1997) made it clear that Internet forums and Internet communication would not be subject to regulation in the same way as the mass media. This case struck down as unconstitutional elements of the CDA which tried to limit the type of material that could appear on the Internet to that which was "decent" because to do so interfered with First Amendment rights. The more recent decision of *Packingham* v. *North Carolina* (2017) confirms that SMCs are viewed as a protected area for free speech. While this decision has been criticized (Citron & Richards, 2018), it remains the law that SMCs cannot be subjected to legislation which purports to limit speech, and thus infringe First Amendment rights.

From a US standpoint, the question of whether to require SMCs to remove hate speech is fairly straightforward. As the United States does not have hate speech laws, coupled with the CDA provisions which grant SMCs immunity from liability as confirmed by *Packingham* v. *Carolina* (2017), for the US government to refuse to impose a requirement on SMCs to remove hate speech, tallies perfectly with the US legal approach to free speech (Beliveau, 2018). Although some US academics have put forward arguments in favor of hate speech restrictions (Beliveau, 2018; Waldron, 2012) and in favor of online regulation (Bridy, 2018; Citron & Wittes, 2017), the situation remains that under current laws, governmental regulation of online hate speech is unlawful. Given that most major SMCs are originally based in Silicon Valley, it stands to reason that US cultural and legal assumptions about free speech will predominate. This is why the starting point for most debates on regulating online speech has been framed by free speech concerns.

However, the starting point from a European perspective is different. Under Article 10 of the European Convention on Human Rights (ECHR), it is possible for a State to create a law that imposes a limit on our freedom of expression so long as under Article 10(2) this law is:

> [...] necessary in a democratic society, in the interests of national security, territorial integrity or public safety, for the prevention of disorder or crime, for the protection of health or morals, for the protection of the reputation or rights of others .... (Art 10, ECHR)

In relation to hate speech, the European Court of Human Rights (ECrtHR) has developed a body of case law which outlines to what extent States can deviate from the basic principle of freedom of expression. There is a line of cases that has advanced a relatively low level of protection for expression that has incited hatred against minorities (*Pavel Ivanov* v. *Russia*, 2007) and gives States wide discretion when it comes to criminalizing or prohibiting such behavior. Although there has been criticism of the ECrtHR's approach because it appears to give less protection to some minorities compared to others, the basic point – that hate speech laws are *prima facie* legitimate – still stands.

While the ECHR does not set out a definition of hate speech, and neither does it compel the enactment of hate speech laws, it has gone as far as recommending that signatory countries review their domestic legislation to ensure that it complies with the need for hate speech provisions, and urges signatories to ratify the International Convention on the Elimination of all Forms of Racial Discrimination, which under Article 4 requires countries to outlaw speech that aims to incite racial hatred (Council of Europe, Committee of Ministers, Recommendation on Hate Speech, 1997). In relation to online hate speech, the Council of Europe's Additional Protocol (Council of Europe, 2002) to the Convention on Cybercrime concerning the criminalization of acts of a racist and xenophobic nature committed through computer systems, goes further than the ECHR which "permits" hate speech laws, by imposing an obligation on signatories to create laws specifically to combat xenophobia and racism generated through computer systems.

Insofar as international human rights frameworks are concerned, freedom of speech is protected by Article 19 of the Universal Declaration of Human Rights and under Article 19 of the International Covenant on Civil and Political Rights (ICCPR). Freedom of speech is fundamental according to these frameworks, but not absolute, and limitations to freedom of speech are articulated under Article 19(3). In addition to these limitations, Article 20(2) of the ICCPR requires that any "advocacy of national, racial, or religious hatred that constitutes incitement to discrimination, hostility or violence" must be prohibited by law. Thus freedom of speech is firmly part of international human rights law and set the outer limits of hate speech laws, but the wide acknowledgment of freedom of speech hides huge discrepancies in how free speech is balanced with hate speech (O'Regan, 2018). The United States in particular has entered a reservation with regard to Article 20 (2).

Most European countries have evolved their own set of hate speech laws that are the result of their own political and cultural history. As such, hate speech laws will vary from country to country such as in terms of which groups are protected by the laws, or how the "hate" is manifested (O'Regan, 2018). Nevertheless, there is a common core to these offences in that they attempt in some way to outlaw speech that incites violence, hatred or discrimination against named groups. Such hate speech offences, therefore, put the onus on European states to enforce them. Since it is frequently impossible to locate and prosecute the speaker of the information, this immediately raises the question whether SMCs as gatekeepers should be liable. SMCs in the EU may be liable under relevant criminal laws if they have knowledge of such speech and omit to take any action under principles of accessorial liability (Coe, 2015).

If we take the US position on hate speech as our starting point, this means that there is a justifiable assumption that the law should not compel SMCs to do anything about this material as to do so would impose unjustifiable restrictions on free speech. Thus, if an argument is to be made for regulation to occur, we would need to put forward a very good explanation for why the material is harmful, and why it needs to be criminalized. While some academics have engaged philosophically with this question (e.g. Waldron, 2012) and researchers have tried to show the harm caused by online hate (e.g. Awan & Zampi, 2015, 2016), it can be difficult to prove categorically a causal link between online and offline hate crime other than in the most extreme cases such as in terrorism-related situations.

By contrast, if the debate were framed more from a European perspective, the question posed would be fundamentally different. Given that the material concerned is already illegal under national laws, the question then becomes why SMCs should *not* be compelled to remove it.

This has led many to raise the question of whether SMCs should take greater responsibility for content on their platforms. For example, a report by the UK Parliament has called for a special category of responsibility to be created under UK law which would see SMCs defined as something between mere "platforms" and publishers, thus, presumably envisaging greater responsibility than mere notice and take-down (Digital, Culture, Media and Sport Committee – House of Commons, "Disinformation and Fake News final report," 2019). This recommendation has now been followed up in the UK Government "Online Harms" White Paper. This has outlined plans to impose a duty of care on SMCs to protect their users from harm (DCMS and Home Department, 2019). The appropriate legal status of SMCs has been explored in detail elsewhere (e.g. Bridy, 2018; Klonick, 2018). However, it is clear that the status quo is being challenged and in ways that do not automatically result in infringements to freedom of expression.

It is important to recognize this difference between the US approach to regulation, and what could be broadly referred to as the European approach. Failing to do so can mean that two important points are lost in the debate. The first is that whether or not a state can legitimately impose legal obligations on SMCs to remove illegal hate material will depend on its approach to free speech as a constitutional right more generally, and hate speech more specifically. Therefore, to oppose regulation purely on the basis of freedom of speech is driven largely by US First Amendment concerns and does not recognize the varying approaches to hate speech across the world.

The second point that is often lost in the debate because of the emphasis on free speech is that there is a crucial difference between regulating legal speech and regulating illegal speech. Any discussion about regulation needs to pay close attention to what is considered illegal hate speech under the law, and cannot be based purely on what might be deemed to be "unacceptable" content, but which may be entirely legal, and which it would not be legitimate to expect SMCs to remove.

Thus, this section has shown that while freedom of expression concerns are legitimate, where hate speech laws already exist, imposing an obligation on SMCs to take more responsibility for content on their site is not controversial as a general principle. However, how this is implemented in practice is crucial. The next section will examine some of the ways currently being used to do this, or where proposals have been put forward to impose greater responsibility on SMCs.

4. OPTIONS FOR REGULATION

So far, we have shown that SMCs are in a position to exert some control over the material on their platforms. We have also shown that while freedom of expression concerns are legitimate, where hate speech laws already exist, imposing an obligation on SMCs to accept more responsibility for their site is not controversial as a general principle. However, how this is implemented in practice is crucial, and overly broad provisions, or ones that do not sufficiently oversee the moderation process, could lead to too much legal material being removed.

In this next section, we will examine two ways in which regulation of hate speech can occur. The first is through self-regulation, and the second is through top-down regulation with an element of co-regulation (Finck, 2018). It will be argued that self-regulation is problematic and not the appropriate way forward. A better approach is through top-down regulation, such as in Germany and the United Kingdom, but in order for this to be successful, it has to be done in such a way that there are appropriate protections in place for freedom of expression. We will also analyze the EU approach to regulation which appears to be moving toward a pro-active filtering model which will require SMCs to use automation, at least to an extent, to keep their platforms safe. This approach is mirrored, in part, by the UK proposals in this area, and suggests that this is the direction in which regulation is moving. This too will bring challenges from a freedom of speech point of view that will require particular attention to be paid to the balancing of the different interests in this area.

4.1. Self-Regulation as a Public Relations Exercise and its Impact on Free Speech – Really a Softer Option?

To begin with, SMCs were reluctant to police the material that appears on their platforms because this interfered with their business model and the concept of net neutrality. However, as it became increasingly clear that their users were concerned by the level of hate that appears on these platforms, SMCs could see that there were business advantages to being seen to take the problem seriously. Even in the United States where freedom of expression concerns are paramount from a legal point of view, research by the Pew Research Centre suggests that 80% of respondents are firmly in favor of SMCs taking responsibility for preventing abuse online, while more than half of respondents said that it was more important that SMCs created a welcoming environment than for people to have the right to say what they want online (Rainie & Anderson, 2017 – Pew Research Centre, 2017). From the SMCs point of view, there has, therefore, been a very clear business case for creating their own rules in relation to what material appears online (Frosio, 2018). As a result, SMCs, such as Facebook and Twitter, have published on their websites acceptable use policies and guidelines which are, essentially, self-regulatory tools to govern "objectionable content." An additional reason why SMCs have been keen to regulate is because it was seen as a way of avoiding governmental interference with their business structures.

There have also been initiatives both in the United States and in Europe to set up voluntary codes of conduct that SMCs sign up to, and which encourage them to remove unlawful material. In the United States, the Working Group on Cyberhate was convened by the American Defamation League (ADL, 2016) to look into developing the most effective responses to online hate and bigotry. They have produced a Best Practices report which tech companies are urged to voluntarily adopt. As we have seen above, the EU has also published its own voluntary code of conduct which it periodically evaluates to test the efficacy of self-regulation.

While SMCs are not state entities, and so, therefore, not subject to First Amendment restrictions in the United States, there are concerns that the size and dominance of these websites, as well as the central role they play in forming public opinion, effectively means that they control citizens' access to speech and so if they block material that is not illegal according to the law, they are creating censorship through the back door. This has raised serious concerns in the United States, particularly amongst free speech advocates and Internet libertarians who have strong beliefs in the importance of a free and neutral Internet. They worry that permitting SMCs to block material at will prevents freedom of expression and curbs innovation (see e.g. discussion in Citron & Richards, 2018). This has led to attempts to impose network neutrality on SMCs through the Open Internet Order 2010 that purported to prohibit SMCs from blocking any material that passes through their website. However, in the landmark case of *Verizon Communications Inc. v. Federal Communications Commission* (2014) the Court of Appeal invalidated certain aspects of the Order and effectively ruled that SMCs could block material on their websites. While *Verizon* does now allow SMCs legally to apply their community standards, a debate continues to rage in the US over whether network neutrality should also apply to them. More recently, the Democrats have introduced the "Save the Internet Act 2019" in a bid to restore aspects of the Order. At the time of writing, this has successfully been passed by the House of Representatives but awaits its fate in the Senate.

This issue is compounded by two further problematic aspects of these guidelines. While SMCs, such as Facebook, are willing to adapt their moderation process at the regional level to include material that happens to be illegal in a particular country (Klonick, 2018), their terms of service which apply to material which is not necessarily illegal, take effect globally. To the extent that the balance is made in the US headquarters of the companies concerned, there is an allegation of US dominance. For example, Facebook seems to be more obsessed with nudity than depictions of extreme violence, a critique which was made in the wake of it taking down an iconic image of a 9-year old girl running away from a napalm attack during the Vietnam War for the reason that it showed "fully nude genitalia." Second, while the guidelines have now been published, they contain, by necessity, general principles which are abstract and whose application in a particular case are opaque.

Thus, while voluntary codes might be viewed as a cheap and fairly easy solution to the problem of online hate, and one which avoids fully fledged legislation, it does give SMCs a great deal of power over what appears online. While freedom of speech advocates have been very critical of proposals in favor of governmental regulation of SMCs, this seems to miss the point that without governmental oversight, self-regulation by the SMCs themselves runs the risk of over-moderation. This potentially poses a bigger risk to freedom of expression than a well thought-out regulatory framework which would limit content removal to material that is unlawful. Furthermore, self-regulation by itself is also not entirely suitable because platform providers are motivated by their own financial and business interests, and, thus, self-regulation lacks transparency and legitimacy insofar as the public interest is concerned.

4.2. Legislative Interventions

As a result of some of the problems associated with self-regulation, some countries have opted for a legislative approach. Germany was the first country to impose fines on SMCs for failing to remove illegal material quickly enough (Frosio, 2018). At the time of writing (September 2020), the Austrian government is in the process of drawing up laws that would fine social media companies up to 10 million Euros if illegal material is not deleted within days. The United Kingdom has put forward proposals for a systematic approach to the regulation of SMCs that differs from the approach adopted in Germany and France. This section will consider the German and UK approaches in more detail.

In April 2019, the UK Government published a White Paper setting out its intention to introduce a legislative framework for minimizing the dissemination of "online harms" on social media. The White Paper deals with a broad spectrum of "online harms" including pornography, terrorist content and child sexual exploitation. Hate speech is not included in the list of online harms, although it can be assumed that the paper has included this with "hate crime" which is within the ambit of the proposals (UK White Paper, 2019). The current UK Government has debated for a while as to how to tackle "harmful" content on social media sites. The White Paper proposes to require technology firms to sign up to a number of Codes of Practice, which impose obligations on SMCs to police content on their site. It is also proposed that a new statutory duty of care will be imposed on SMCs, and that a new regulator will be created. This regulator will have the power to fine and issue sanctions against senior executives, and the power to disrupt through the obligations imposed on ancillary services such as search engines and payment providers, and to order blocking at Internet access level (UK White Paper, 2019). Thus, the UK White Paper goes far beyond a notice and take-down obligation for SMCs as hosting providers and will impose a variety of obligations both on SMCs themselves as well as third parties. SMCs themselves will have an obligation to take pro-active measures to police their sites by using automated filtering and content recognition technologies. Both the vagueness of the regulations imposed by the regulator and the breadth of the scope of measures and the fact that these measures will apply not only to illegal content, but also to "unacceptable" content causes great concern about freedom of expression. Although the White Paper does mention safeguards such as transparency, accountability and complaints procedures, these may not be sufficient.

While it is not surprising in the current climate that the UK government is seeking to impose legal obligations on SMCs to ensure that illegal content does not appear on their sites, it is concerning that the White Paper is not precise in its treatment of hate speech. To begin with, it is particularly problematic that "hate speech" is, we assume, simply subsumed into the category of "hate crime" without any recognition of the different issues relating to the two in this context. While "hate crime" can be used as a broad category that can include "hate speech," it is important to understand that in this context, "hate speech" is different to other "hate crimes" in one important respect. Hate speech is characterized by the fact that it makes certain types of *speech* illegal based on its *content*, whereas, generally speaking, other types of hate crime deal with *behavior* that is already illegal (such as assault or criminal damage), but which is aggravated on the basis that the perpetrator was motivated by or demonstrated hostility toward a protected characteristic. This means that freedom of speech concerns are central to any treatment of "hate speech" offences, whereas of less concern in relation to other types of hate crime. As such, to ensure that our freedom of expression is properly protected, SMCs would need very clear guidance on what material they can remove and what material they should not remove. This issue is compounded by the fact that the statutory duty of care envisaged under the White Paper, would not only apply in respect of content that is illegal under UK laws, but also to "unacceptable content" that is offensive but legal. The use of such vague terminology does little to assuage any fears that SMCs will find it more expedient to over-moderate to be sure they satisfy their duty of care, than to under-moderate and risk breaking the law. At the time of writing, the UK government has put proposals before Parliament to create a new online regulatory body.

While the UK proposals could be termed ambitious and all-encompassing, by contrast, the German Act focuses specifically on improving the speed and efficiency of notice and take-down and is, therefore, far more limited in scope. The German legislative proposals do not impose any obligations to pro-actively filter content as to do so was seen as contrary to the hosting immunity contained in Article 14 and the prohibition on a general obligation to monitor in Article 15 of the E-commerce Directive 2000/31/EC. Arguably the obligations of SMCs to monitor online content as imposed by the duty of care in the UK White Paper may conflict with Articles 14 and 15 (which may or may not apply to the United Kingdom by the time the legislation is enacted).

In Germany, like the United Kingdom, politicians have blamed social media providers for contributing to the dissemination of hate speech online and have called on them to "do more" to prevent the spread of hate speech, abuse and extremist content on their platforms. In this vein, the German Minister of Justice, Heiko Maas, published a draft Bill on March 17, 2017 which was passed on September 1, 2017 and came into force on October 1, 2017 (Network Law Enforcement Act, 2017). In the speech introducing the Bill to Parliament, the German Minister said:

> self-regulation by the relevant companies has had some success, but has been insufficient. New figures show: not enough criminal content is taken down and the processes are too slow. The biggest problem remains that social networks do not take seriously the complaints of their own users. Therefore, it is clear to us that we have to increase the pressure on social networks …. (Maas Speech, 2017)

This Act obliges SMCs with a user base of at least two million users in Germany to take down content infringing a list of certain provisions of the German Criminal Code within 24 hours (for obviously infringing content) or 7 days (where infringement is not immediately obvious), and provide an accessible and efficient notice and take-down procedure for German users, failing which companies may be fined up to 50 million euros (Frosio, 2018; Guggenberger, 2017). This proposal was motivated by the perception of an unacceptable avalanche in hate crime, online abuse and fake news not being countered effectively by SMCs. The Act also introduced bi-annual reporting obligations on SMCs to enhance transparency about user complaints and take-downs, and to put in place a complaints procedure where users can complain about content which has not been taken down. In 2018, the independent complaints body received 8,617 cases, but found only 3,096 justified as content which should be taken down (36%). Only 2% of the cases of illegal content (62) related to racist online hate (Eco Annual Report, 2019). Thus, transparency is one of the standards imposed by newer forms of regulation. However, the German legislation does not force SMCs to provide granular reports on the type of speech which has been removed which would be required to assess the operation of the Act in practice (O'Regan, 2018).

While so far, SMCs have appeared to be judicious in their application of the law Echison & Knodt, 2018, the fact remains that the primary obligation of the SMCs is to remove material rather than to protect freedom of expression. The law itself does not highlight the importance of freedom of expression, and there appears to be no penalty imposed on SMCs if they over-moderate.

The absence of clear protection for freedom of expression, both in the German Law and in the UK White Paper, leaves those attempts open to criticism from freedom of speech advocates. It is possible both to impose a legal obligation on SMCs to remove illegal material and to protect freedom of speech. However, neither attempt analyzed here has done so with the necessary rigor and force.

4.3. EU Law Shifting Away from Intermediary Immunity by Imposing Technological Monitoring Obligations

As has already been observed, until about 2016, the main approach for dealing with illegal content on SMCs' sites was reliance on self-regulatory Codes of Conduct. At the EU level, this manifested itself in the EU Code of Conduct on countering illegal hate speech online which was initiated by the Commission and which was initially joined by Facebook, Microsoft, YouTube and Twitter, with more SMCs joining in 2018. The EU Commission claims in its 4th Monitoring Round of the operation of this self-regulatory Code of Conduct that 89% of content flagged/reported was reviewed within 24 hours and that 72% of content alleged by users and relevant organizations to be illegal hate speech was actually removed (EU Commissioner for Justice, Consumers and Gender Equality, 2019). More specifically, YouTube removed 85% of such content, Facebook 82%, but Twitter only 44%. As to feedback to users and transparency, on an average, 65% of user notification received feedback from the relevant SMC: Facebook 93%, Twitter 60% and YouTube only in 25% of notifications. The reason for this may be that YouTube is placing reliance on its trusted flaggers programme to which it provides feedback, but not to normal users. Google+ does not provide any feedback in response to notifications (EU Commissioner for Justice, Consumers and Gender Equality, 2019).

However, the recent spate of terror attacks within the EU has changed the purely self-regulatory, laissez-faire approach, and this change is beginning to be reflected in EU instruments countering illegal content. While EU law prevents Member States from imposing liability for illegal content on SMCs before they have actual or constructive knowledge of illegal content on their sites, authorities or courts can order intermediaries to prevent or terminate an infringement or establish a procedure for removing or disabling access to information according to Article 15 of the E-commerce Directive 2000/31/EC. Thus while the starting point is a general immunity for Internet intermediaries, various EU legal instruments have recently qualified this immunity. As a result, while initially EU instruments in this area advocated self-regulation and abstaining from the use of automated detection tools, this approach is now changing with a move toward regulatory measures and the use of (at least partially) automated content moderation.

The Counter-Terrorism Directive (2017) imposes an obligation on EU Member States to ensure the prompt take-down of "online content constituting a public provocation to commit a terrorist offence" (Article 21(1)), and where this is not possible, they may provide for Internet access blocking of such content (Article 21(3)) subject to transparent procedures and adequate safeguards (Article 21(3)). The Directive explicitly does not impose an obligation to seek out prohibited content, for example, through automated means using artificial intelligence, but leaves the active policing of their platforms to SMCs through self-regulation. It also limits states' legal intervention to ensuring take-down occurs (Recitals 22–23). This aligns with the EU approach to online media regulation in the latest reiteration of the Audio-Visual Media Services Directive (AVMS) (EU Directive, 2018), which included video-sharing platforms for the first time within the scope of regulation. SMCs are included in the category of video-sharing platforms if the sharing of videos is not merely an ancillary or minor part of the functionality they offer (Recital 5, Art 1 (1) (aa)).

The AVMS Directive envisages and encourages the drawing up of Codes of Conduct by the video-sharing platforms (Art 4a (1) and (2)), but it advocates a co-regulatory approach, beyond the self-regulatory approach. Member States must establish (a) regulator(s) to assess the measures taken by the video-sharing platforms themselves (Art 28b (5)).

First, Article 28b stipulates that EU Member States must take positive measures to ensure protection from three types of content. Second, the general public must be protected from user-generated videos and advertising that contains incitement to violence or hatred against a protected group (Art 21 and Art 28(b) of the EU Charter of Fundamental Rights). Third, the general public must additionally be protected from three types of content prohibited in EU criminal law instruments contained in user-generated videos and advertisements: (1) public provocation to commit a terrorist offence (Counter-Terrorism Directive, 2017), (2) child pornography (Directive on Combatting the Sexual Abuse and Sexual Exploitation of Children, 2011) and (3) offences related to racism and xenophobia (Council Framework Decision on Racism and Xenophobia, 2008). Member States may impose stricter measures, additionally regulating other types of content, thus, the AVMS Directive does not fully harmonize the standards in this area.

Thus, the EU Member States, once the implementation deadline for the AVMS Directive has passed on September 19, 2020, have to take *regulatory* measures to curb online hate speech, terrorist content and child sex abuse material on video-sharing services. The AVMS Directive does not stipulate the precise nature of the measures to be taken by the Member States, but sets out the general principles for taking such measures which are similar to the principles set out in the UK White Paper. First of all, Member States should adopt a risk-based approach, being informed by the nature of the content and its harmfulness, the intended audience to be protected, as well as the interests of the video-sharing platform, the users who have uploaded the content and the public interest. Furthermore the AVMS Directive adopts a practical and proportionate approach which takes into account the size of the video-sharing platform and the nature of its service. Interestingly, the AVMS Directive states that the measures should not comprise "ex-ante control measures" or "upload-filtering of content" in breach of the prohibition on the imposition of general monitoring obligations on hosting services (E-commerce Directive, Article 15(1)). In other words, automated tools based on artificial intelligence must not be implemented in such a way that they lead to the automated, overbroad filtering of content and general monitoring of all content. This means that such tools must be supplemented by human review and the measures themselves must be specific and targeted, in accordance with Article 14 (3) of the E-commerce Directive which permits specific orders by administrative authorities or courts to terminate or prevent an infringement and which also permits procedures "governing the removal or disabling of access to information." Under Article 28b, the AVMS Directive lists the measures which video-sharing platforms must implement by way of co-regulation, such as prohibiting the three types of content in their terms and conditions, providing for users the opportunity to report and flag such illegal content, providing transparent information as to what the SMC has done with content reported or flagged, providing age-verification mechanisms for content harmful to children, implementing content rating systems. parental control systems for content harmful to children, complaints handling measures and measures to improve digital literacy. Furthermore the AVMS Directive envisages the use of alternative dispute resolution mechanisms. Finally, the AVMS Directive envisages further Codes of Conduct in respect of hate speech. While the United Kingdom may not be part of the EU in 2020, the UK White Paper strongly aligns with the approach in the AVMS Directive.

A similar co-regulatory approach (Codes of Conduct coupled with an obligation to implement these standards by SMCs) has been adopted in respect of copyright infringement and this also means that SMCs have to use technological solutions to prevent copyright infringement (such as the prevention of re-uploading of proscribed content previously found through YouTube's content id, or the closure of accounts) in the recent revision of the EU Copyright Directive, which has been similarly controversial (Reynolds, 2019). This Copyright Directive also forces SMC to take on more responsibility in respect of law infringements by user-uploaded content.

Finally, the EU has issued several instruments on measures to effectively tackle illegal content online. The EU Commission's Communication (2017) on tackling illegal content online outlines the Commission's thinking in respect of achieving enhanced responsibility of online platforms for illegal content such as incitement to terrorism, xenophobic and racist speech, and child sex abuse materials and responds to the EU Council's political calls for industry to develop "technology and tools to improve the automatic detection and removal of content" (European

Commission Communication, 2017). The Communication states that SMCs should take pro-active steps to detect and remove illegal content through automated means, but that this currently requires final vetting through human review (which it calls the "human-in-the-loop" principle). The EU Commission points to the need to ensure notice and stay-down of illegal content, and in particular, the need to prevent re-uploads of the same known content by automatic means.

Moreover, it points to the need for close co-operation between SMCs and law enforcement, but also between law enforcement authorities within the EU to achieve a better co-ordinated response and refers to the EU Internet Referral Unit at Europol as a model of EU co-operation. It points to the greater effectiveness of notice and take-down schemes using trusted flaggers (such as the IRU at Europol) and recommends EU-wide criteria and certification of trusted flagger schemes to prevent abuse of take-down mechanisms and to protect freedom of expression. Furthermore all users should have available convenient and easy-to-use reporting mechanisms. The Communication points to the need to preserve the evidence of criminal activity (and share it with law enforcement). Finally, the EU Commission calls for increased transparency about the number and types of notices received, the time it took to respond to the notices, and any actions taken. In addition, the Community Guidelines and procedures for notice and action should be transparent, and the Commission recommends the availability of counter-notices contesting removal of content.

The Communication was followed up with a non-binding EU Commission Recommendation (2018) on measure to effectively tackle illegal content online.

Finally, the EU has issued a Regulation for creating a harmonized system of removal orders for online *terrorist* content (EU Regulation on preventing the dissemination of terrorist content online, 2018). The EU Commission Proposal envisages a new removal order for terrorist content (any format, not just videos, but also images and text) on hosting services, including social media. This would apply to all hosting platforms, regardless of their size and introduce co-ordination obligations between the authorities of the Member States and Europol and sets as a standard that terrorist content must be removed by SMCs within 1 hour. The Proposal also provides that SMCs must use automated detection tools, but envisages safeguards, complaints mechanisms and transparency reporting. In particular, Article 9 (2) currently provides that

> Safeguards shall consist, in particular, of human oversight and verifications where appropriate and, in any event, where a detailed assessment of the relevant context is required to determine whether or not the content is to be considered terrorist content.

Finally, it provides for the preservation of content taken down, to enable the investigation and prosecution of criminal offences, or if content is found not to be illegal, to enable it to be uploaded again.

Thus, it can be seen that both the UK and the EU approaches are moving away from notice and take-down, and toward pro-active filtering. This brings with it particular issues in relation to freedom of expression that will need to be at the heart of any such initiatives. Coe points to the social media paradox – the fact that social media open up unprecedented opportunities for the free flow of speech, and, thus, user empowerment, but that this empowerment is equally dangerous and threatens individual rights and public disorder (Coe, 2015). It is this paradox which calls for the finding of an appropriate balance between the protection of free speech and the prohibition of hate speech. There are huge challenges ahead, and to steer a path that balances the different interests at stake will require compromise and cooperation.

5. WAYS OF TACKLING HATE SPEECH OTHER THAN HARD LAW OR SELF-REGULATION

It seems clear, therefore, that while platform providers do have at their disposal the technology and money to do something to help combat online hate speech, there are important limitations to the effectiveness of these remedies. Shifting the responsibility to third party intermediaries is a cheap and politically expedient solution, but it is important to recognize that it will not be a panacea.

There are different types and levels of hate speech. The motivation of the maker of the hate speech can range from the unthinking and thoughtless, to the purposeful and intentionally destructive. The impact of the hate speech could be just as serious irrespective of the intention of the offender, however, it may make a difference to how SMCs deal with that behavior, particularly when dealing with the makers of hate speech who are on the lower end of the spectrum of seriousness (Bakalis, 2017; Rowbottom, 2012).

Researchers have found that people behave differently depending on a variety of factors such as anonymity and incentives for good behavior (Binns, 2014). For example, there is evidence that those sites which encourage anonymity have far greater incidences of bullying and hate speech (Binns, 2013).

Furthermore, one problem is the "filter bubble," which means that because of the profit-maximizing architecture of most social media sites, content is targeted on the basis of profiles of users' interest as this maximizes users' engagement with the social media site and therefore advertising revenues (Pariser, 2011). But as a consequence, user groups are segregated into different groups, for example, in relation to their political or religious identity. This in turn means that users do not challenge their own views and opinions against those of others which leads to echo chambers and increases the likelihood of users expressing hate. This again is a problem stemming from the architecture of social media sites. The major SMCs, such as Facebook and Twitter, have, therefore, launched specific counter-speech initiatives to challenge those users who seem to be interested in extremist content.

Other potential ways of discouraging hate speech could be by allowing victims of hate speech to confront the person that has written something about them to explain why what they have said is harmful. Or by encouraging the use of the technology that already exists on SMCs, such as Twitter, which allows users to block material from their view or to silence it without Twitter having to remove the offending material. There are also preventative measures that should be considered, and which could be used to prevent unlawful material appearing in the first place. For instance, codes of conduct can provide clearer guidelines to users about what kind of conduct is considered unacceptable by giving examples of the sorts of speech that can fall foul of the law.

6. CONCLUSION

Evidently, SMCs do have the technological know-how to help in the fight against online hate, at least to some extent. However, the rhetoric in relation to regulation of online hate has tended to be dominated by US First Amendment concerns, which do not represent the legal culture in other areas of the world, such as Europe. It is, therefore, legitimate for a state to compel SMCs to remove online hate if to do so aligns with its legal stance on hate speech and with its position on Internet regulation more broadly.

However, it is important that any attempt to do so makes clear distinctions between legal material (which should not be removed) and illegal material (which can be removed). Attempts to impose legal responsibilities on SMCs in Germany and the United Kingdom, while different in their respective approaches, fall short of this.

Given that the EU position appears to be shifting toward imposing greater responsibility on SMCs, including the potential to require them to act proactively in relation to illegal material, this issue is pressing. As well as some of the conceptual concerns identified in this piece about the difference between legal and illegal hate speech, the issue of proactivity and reactivity and the appropriate legal status of SMCs, we also need to consider whether there are other ways in which SMCs can be forced to act, for example, by finding ways to actively discourage hate speech on their platforms through measures with less impact on freedom of expression. Content moderation through technology is also a major concern for free speech as it makes regulation non-transparent, inaccurate and unaccountable.

NOTE

1. Netzwerkdurchsuchungsgesetz, NetzDG.

REFERENCES

American Defamation League. (2016). Best practices for responding to cyberhate. Retrieved from https://www.adl.org/best-practices-for-responding-to-cyberhate

Ammar, J. (2019). Cyber Gremlin: Social networking machine learning, and the global war on Al-Qaida and IS-inspired terrorism. *International Journal of Law and Information Technology*, 27(3), 238–265.

Amnesty International. (2019). Troll patrol findings. Retrieved from https://decoders.amnesty.org/projects/troll-patrol/findings#what_did_we_find_container

Association for Canadian Studies, and Canadian Race Relations Foundation. (2019). Canadians views on hate Retrieved from https://www.crrf-fcrr.ca/en/resources/research-projects/item/26994-canadian-views-on-hatred-national-survey-to-be-released-to-mark-international-day-for-the-prevention-of-racial-discrimination.

Awan, I., & Zempi, I. (2015). 'I will blow your face off' – Virtual and physical world anti-Muslim hate crime. *British Journal of Criminology 57*(2), 362–380. doi:10.1093/bjc/azv122

Awan, I., & Zempi, I. (2016). The affinity between online and offline anti-Muslim hate crime: Dynamics and impacts. *Aggression and Violent Behaviour*, *27*, 1–8.

Bakalis, C. (2017). Rethinking cyberhate laws. *Information and Communications Technology Law*, *27*, 86.

BBC News (1). (2019). Retrieved from https://www.bbc.co.uk/news/technology-47758455

BBC News (2). (2019). Retrieved from https://www.bbc.co.uk/news/world-asia-48033313

Beliveau, A. (2018). Hate speech laws in the United States and the council of Europe: The fine balance between protecting individual freedom of expression rights and preventing the rise of extremism and radicalization through social media sites. *Suffolk University Law Review*, *51*(4), 565–588.

Binns, A. (2013). Facebook's ugly sisters: Anonymity and abuse on Formspring and Ask.fm. *Media Education Research Journal*, ISSN, 2040–4530. https://www.academia.edu/4298024/Facebooks_Ugly_Sisters_Anonymity_and_Abuse_on_Ask_fm_and_Formspring_me

Binns, A. (2014). Twitter city and Facebook village: Teenage girls' personas and experiences influenced by choice architecture in social networking sites. *Journal of Media Practice*, *15*(2), 71.

Boyd, D., & Ellison, N. (2007). Social network sites: Definition, history and scholarship. *Journal of Computer-mediated Communication*, *13*, 210–230.

Bridy, A. (2018). Remediating social media: A layer-conscious approach. *Boston University Journal of Science and Technology Law*, *24*, 193.

Citron, D. K., & Richards, N. M. (2018). Four principles for digital expression (You Won't Believe #3!). *Washington University Law Review*, *95*, 1353.

Citron, D. K., & Wittes, B. (2017). The Internet will not break: Denying bad Samaritans Section 230 immunity. *Fordham Law Review*, *86*(2), 401.

Coe, P. (2015). The social media paradox 24 (1). *Information & Communications Technology Law*, *24*(1), 16–40.

Cohen-Almagor, R. (2015). *Confronting the Internet's dark side: Moral and social responsibility on the free highway*. Cambridge: Cambridge University Press.

Commission Staff Working Document. (2018). Impact Assessment, Proposal for a Regulation of the European Parliament and of the Council on Preventing the Dissemination of Terrorist Content Online. SWD(2018) 408 final of 12 September 2018, p. 14.

Commission Staff Working Document. (2019). Impact Assessment, Proposal for a Regulation of the European Parliament and of the Council on Preventing the Dissemination of Terrorist Content Online. SWD(2018) 408 final of 12 September 2019, p. 15.

Council Framework Decision on Racism and Xenophobia. (2008). 2008/913/JHA of 28th November 2008.

Council of Europe. (2002). Additional protocol to the convention on cybercrime concerning the criminalisation of acts of a racist and xenophobic nature committed through computer systems. Retrieved from https://rm.coe.int/168008160f

Council of Europe, Committee of Ministers. (1997). Recommendation R (97) 20 of the Committee of Ministers to Members States on "Hate Speech".

Digital, Culture, Media and Sport Committee. (2019). *Disinformation and fake news final report*. House of Commons, 8th Report of Session 2017-19, 2019.

Eco Annual Report. (2019). Retrieved from https://www.eco.de/wp-content/uploads/2019/03/20190310_Jahresbericht_Beschwerdestelle_2018.pdf and https://www.zeit.de/politik/deutschland/2019-03/netzdg-netzwerkdurchsetzungsgesetz-jahresbericht-eco-beschwerdestelle

Echison, W., & Knodt, O. (2018). *Germany's NetzDG: A key test for combatting online hate*. CEPS Research Report no. 2018/9.

EU Commission's Communication. (2017). COM(2017) 555 final of 28 September 2017. Retrieved from https://www.isdc.ch/media/1579/2-https___eur-lexeuropa.pdf

EU Commissioner for Justice, Consumers and Gender Equality. (2019). Factsheet. Retrieved from https://ec.europa.eu/info/policies/justice-and-fundamental-rights/combatting-discrimination/racism-and-xenophobia/countering-illegal-hate-speech-online_en

EU Voluntary Code of Conduct. (2016). Retrieved from https://ec.europa.eu/info/policies/justice-and-fundamental-rights/combatting-discrimination/racism-and-xenophobia/countering-illegal-hate-speech-online_en

Finck, M. (2018). Digital co-regulation: Designing a supranational legal framework for the platform economy. *European Law Review, 43*(1), 47–68.

Frosio, G. (2018). Why keep a dog and bark yourself? From intermediary liability to re-sponsibility. *International Journal of Law and Information Technology, 26*(1), 1–33.

Guardian News (1). (2018). Retrieved from https://www.theguardian.com/technology/2018/sep/24/facebook-moderators-mental-trauma-lawsuit

Guardian News (2). (2018). Facebook releases content moderation guidelines – Rules long kept secret. Retrieved from https://www.theguardian.com/technology/2018/apr/24/facebook-releases-content-moderation-guidelines-secret-rules

Guardian Newspaper. (2018). Cambridge Analytica files. Retrieved from https://www.theguardian.com/news/series/cambridge-analytica-files

Guggenberger, N. (2017). Das Netzwerkdurchsetzungsgesetz in der Anwendung. *Neue Juristische Wochenschrift, 70*(36), 2577–2582.

Johnson, D., & Post, D. (1996). Law and borders: The rise of law in cyberspace. *Stanford Law Review, 48*(5), 1367.

Klonick, K. (2018). The new governors: The people, rules and processes governing online speech. *Harvard Law Review, 131*, 1598.

Laidlaw, E. (2015). *Regulating speech in cyberspace.* Cambridge: Cambridge University Press.

Lessig, L. (1999). *Code and other laws of cyberspace.* New York, NY: Basic Books.

Maas Speech. (2017). Retrieved from http://www.bmjv.de/SharedDocs/Artikel/DE/2017/03142017_GE_Rechtsdurchsetzung_Soziale_Netzwerke.html

Murray, A. (2007). *The regulation of cyberspace: Control in the online environment.* New York, NY: Routledge.

Murray, A. (2016). *Information technology law* (3rd ed.). Oxford: Oxford University Press.

O'Regan, C. (2018). Hate speech online: An (intractable) contemporary challenge? *Current Legal Problems, 71*(1), 403–429.

Pariser, E. (2011). *The filter bubble: How the new personalized Web is changing what we read and how we think.* London: Penguin.

Rainie, L., & Anderson, J. (2017). *The fate of online trust in the next decade.* Pew Research Center. Retrieved from http://assets.pewresearch.org/wp-content/uploads/sites/14/2017/08/09163223/PI_2017.08.10_onlineTrustNextDecade_FINAL.pdf [https://perma.cc/YK8P-ABYU]

Reynolds, M. (2019). What is Article 13? The EU's divisive new copyright plan explained. *Wired.* Retrieved from https://www.wired.co.uk/article/what-is-article-13-article-11-european-directive-on-copyright-explained-meme-ban

Rowbottom, J. (2012). To rant, vent and converse: Protecting low level digital speech. *Cambridge Law Journal, 71*, 355.

Secretary of State for Digital, Culture, Media & Sport and the Secretary of State for the Home Department. (2019). Online Harms White Paper Retrieved from https://www.gov.uk/government/consultations/online-harms-white-paper.

Süddeutsche Report. (2016). Retrieved from https://www.sueddeutsche.de/digital/exklusive-sz-magazin-recherche-inside-facebook-1.3297138

The Cleaners Documentary. (2018). Retrieved from https://www.theverge.com/2018/1/21/16916380/sundance-2018-the-cleaners-movie-review-facebook-google-twitter

UN General Assembly. (2018). Report of the UN Special Rapporteur David Kaye on the Promotion and Protection of the Right to Freedom of Opinion and Expression. A/HRC/38/35.

US Senate Committee on Commerce, Science and Transportation. (2018). Hearing on extremist propaganda and social media. Retrieved from https://www.c-span.org/video/?439849-1/facebook-twitter-youtube-officials-testify-combating-extremism

Waldron, J. (2012). *The harm in hate speech.* Cambridge, MA: Harvard University Press.

Wired. (2018). Retrieved from https://www.wired.co.uk/article/isis-propaganda-home-office-algorithm-asi

Zuckerberg, M. (2019). Retrieved from https://www.independent.co.uk/news/world/americas/mark-zuckerberg-facebook-regulation-internet-government-washington-post-a8847701.html (original *Washington Post* article is behind a pay-wall).

Cases, Statutes and EU Directives/Regulations

ACLU v. *Reno* (1997) – 521 U.S. 844 (1997).

Audio-Visual Media Services Directive (EU) 2018/1808 of 14th November 2018.

Brandenburg v. *Ohio*, 395 U.S. 444 (1969). In the case of *R.A.V. v. City of St Paul*, 505 U.S. 377 (1992).

Combatting the Sexual Abuse and Sexual Exploitation of Children Directive 2011/93/EU.

EU Commission (2017) COM(2017) 555 final of 28 September 2017, p. 16.

Commission Recommendation of 1 March 2018, C(2018) 1177 (final).

Counter-Terrorism Directive (EU) 2017/541.

E-commerce Directive 2000/31/EC.

EU Charter of Fundamental Rights.

EU Directive Copyright in the Digital Single Market.

EU Regulation on preventing the dissemination of terrorist content online, 2018 Proposal of 19 September 2018, COM/2018/640 final.

Network Law Enforcement Act 2017. Retrieved from http://www.bmjv.de/SharedDocs/Gesetzgebungsverfahren/DE/NetzDG.html (in German).

Pavel Ivanov v. *Russia*, Application no. 35222/04 (2007).

Packingham v. *North Carolina* 137 S. Ct. 1730 (2017).

The Counter-Terrorism Directive (EU) 2017/541 on Combating Terrorism of 15th March 2017.

Verizon Communications Inc. v. *Federal Communications* Commission 740 F.3d 623 (D.C. Cir. 2014).

CHAPTER 5

A SOCIO-LEGAL ANALYSIS OF GENDER-BASED VICTIMIZATION, MISOGYNY AND THE HATE CRIME PARADIGM IN ENGLAND AND WALES

Marian Duggan

ABSTRACT

In England and Wales, legislation pertaining to hate crime recognizes hostility based on racial identity, religious affiliation, sexual orientation, disability or transgender identity. Discussions abound as to whether this legislation should also recognize hostility based on gender or misogyny. Taking a socio-legal analysis, the chapter examines hate crime, gender-based victimization and misogyny alongside the impact of victim identity construction, access to justice and the international nature of gendered harm. The chapter provides a comprehensive investigation of gender-based victimization in relation to targeted hostility to assess the potential for its inclusion in hate crime legislation in England and Wales.

Keywords: Gender hostility; hate crime; violence against women; law reform; victims; identity

INTRODUCTION

In 2018, the Law Commission for England and Wales began reviewing the adequacy and parity of legal protections around hate crime. Two key areas of

Studies in Law, Politics, and Society, Volume 85, 101–128
Copyright © 2021 by Emerald Publishing Limited
All rights of reproduction in any form reserved
ISSN: 1059-4337/doi:10.1108/S1059-433720210000085006

potential reform included inequalities among the currently recognized protected characteristics of race, religion, sexual orientation, disability and transgender identity (an issue previously identified in their 2013 review), and potentially including new characteristics such as sex, gender, age, or physical attributes. The Law Commission review sought to understand how particular characteristics should be determined, what the threshold of hostile criminal behaviors might be, and how any changes to existing legislation might affect the concept of hate crime itself. As this chapter will explore, the potential inclusion of sex or gender as a recognized ground for hostility is a welcome development for tackling gender-based victimization and violence against women, however whether this alone will have a realistic impact on reducing gendered victimization is questionable.

Hate crime has been described as "a concept which has inspired legal and social change designed to protect people from being persecuted simply because of who they are, or who they are perceived to be" (Chakraborti, 2015, p. 13). Hate crimes often stem from prejudice toward a group or individual whose identity has been subject to negative rhetoric or ideology by dominant members of society (Lyons, 2006). In the global north, the term has rapidly become a useful shorthand way of referring to targeted victimization fueled by hate, hostility, bias or prejudice and their related criminal offences (Chakraborti & Garland, 2009; Perry, 2001). Perry (2001, p. 10) offers the following useful and informative definition that has become commonplace as a starting point of analysis in hate crime scholarship:

> [Hate Crime] involves acts of violence and intimidation, usually directed toward already stigmatized and marginalized groups. As such, it is a mechanism of power, intended to reaffirm the precarious hierarchies that characterize a given social order. It attempts to recreate simultaneously the threatened (real or imagined) hegemony of the perpetrator's group and the "appropriate" subordinate identity of the victim's group. It is a means of marking both the Self and the Other in such a way as to re-establish their "proper" relative positions, as given and reproduced by broader ideologies and patterns of social and political inequality.

The underlying motive and inherent power dynamics displayed in crimes motivated by hostility or prejudice differentiate them from regular crimes. Victims are often members of, or affiliated to, a subordinated and stigmatized group, while perpetrators often occupy a more dominant identity or status in relation to their victim(s) (Lyons, 2006). However, the identity of the aggressor is often irrelevant to the hostile motivation of the crime; rather, it is the victim (or any other person) who subjectively determines whether they are being subject to hostility based on their identity. Here, the power to ascertain and report an offence as a *hate* crime lies with the victim. The rationale for this, and the broad operational definition employed by the police, is to instill confidence in victims to report incidents where they otherwise might not have done so.

The relevant laws may all refer to hostility rather than hate, but they differ slightly to account for cultural variances (see Chakraborti & Garland, 2009; Hall, 2013; Schweppe, 2012). Northern Ireland and Scotland additionally recognize Sectarianism, but Northern Ireland does not recognize gender identity (i.e. transphobia) as grounds for hate (Duggan, 2013, 2014). Merseyside Police in England and Wales were the first force to recognize sex workers as a protected group and record hate crimes against them accordingly (Campbell, 2016, 2018).

Subsequently, North Yorkshire Police adopted this approach, while Greater Manchester Police choose to record crimes committed against people from alternative subcultures. In July 2016, Nottinghamshire Police became the first UK force to treat misogynistic street harassment as a form of hate crime, following research undertaken by Nottingham Citizens Advice that claimed 38% of women respondents had experienced a hate crime and felt in part that it related to their gender (Nottingham Citizens, 2014). Increasingly, police forces are following Nottinghamshire's lead in recording hate crimes based on either gender or misogyny according to the individual force (Mason-Bish & Duggan, 2019; Mullany & Trickett, 2018). Awareness about the significant similarities between hate crime victimization and violence against women or gender-based violence means the academic debate around "gender hate crime" predates these recent activities (Gill & Mason-Bish, 2013; Mason-Bish & Duggan, 2019). As the topic has been placed on policymakers' agendas once again through the Law Commission's review, a revived exploration of the broader issue is fitting.

The chapter begins with an overview of how hate crime legislation currently operates in England and Wales, examining the rationales for different types of protections. Of importance here is the role identity politics played in creating demarcated hate crime categories which then became hierarchized. This inequality informs wider debates among scholars, policymakers and practitioners about differential treatment between hate crimes and toward victims. This assessment of emergent hierarchies is informed by perspectives on harm and notions of victim (un)deservedness. Examining how this impacts upon victims' access to justice and recognition, the chapter unpacks the socio-legal construction of victims and victimhood. In doing so, it demonstrates how early (male) scholars determined victim "legitimacy," where identity and gender featured heavily in the production, application and rejection of knowledge and "expertise." Drawing on the broader victimological literature, the chapter explores the shifting positionality of crime victims in liberal social and political systems, alongside a gendered consideration of the backlash against the role of culpability, blameworthiness and legitimacy in determining a person's victim status.

Global academic and professional insight into violence against women has significantly expanded since the mid-twentieth century, with a wealth of gender-based research, theory, policy and practice spanning domestic and international domains. As the more recent "hate crimes paradigm" gains greater recognition and acceptance, feminist scholars have begun to explore the law's potential for reducing gender-based violence or violence against women; namely, what – if any – differences it can offer in terms of criminal justice system experiences, responses, redress or punishments. This is of interest due to the current discussions around specificity – in this case, whether to address *misogyny* rather than *gender* in any extended hate crime provisions to better recognize that women are disproportionately subject to hostility (from men). Manne (2017, p. 19) asserts that misogyny has shifted from being commonly understood as an individualized, pathologized phenomenon affiliated to lone persons, to be considered as "serving to uphold patriarchal order [and] understood as one strand among various similar systems of domination." Prioritizing misogyny as a categorization, rather than gender, is considered necessary to recognize the particular dangers, victimization and vulnerabilities women are exposed to as a result of patriarchal oppression on both individual and structural levels (Gill & Mason-Bish, 2013; Mason-Bish & Duggan, 2019). Inherent complexities therefore exist when seeking to address gender hostility or misogyny within the current (regimented) hate crime framework.

To demonstrate these complexities and limitations more clearly, the chapter presents two case studies. The first critically addresses the specific intersectionality of gender and sexuality that manifests in structural and interpersonal acts of violence against women who identify as other than heterosexual, highlighting the limiting nature of "siloing" model of hate crime compartmentalization. The second critically explores the nature and impact of online misogyny that is increasingly manifesting on a global scale due to the rapid expansion of technology-enabled communication. The analysis contained within each demonstrates how legal responses should recognize the gendered specificities of targeted violence against women, but proceed with careful consideration and implementation to avoid exacerbating social hostilities. Finally, the chapter concludes by providing insight into necessary areas for consideration regarding gender, misogyny and hate crime.

THE HATE CRIME LEGISLATIVE FRAMEWORK IN ENGLAND AND WALES

In countries that recognize hate crime and legislate accordingly, variations in approach often link to societal demographics and socio-political contexts, with most indicating intolerance of prejudice-motivated harm by ascribing to a penalty enhancement model. The Office for Democratic Institutions and Human Rights (ODIHR, 2009) suggests that hate crime policy should refer to "current social problems as well as potential historical oppression and discrimination," although countries that adhere to their protocols not bound to this guidance (p. 38). In England and Wales, hate crime legislation recognizes *hostility* and refers to the specific identity characteristics of race, religion, sexual orientation, disability and transgender identity. Legislation differentiates between offences "aggravated" by racial or religious hostility, offences in which hostility (toward any of the five characteristics) can be grounds for "enhanced" sentencing powers, and offences of "stirring up" hatred. Scholars have noted criticism, concern and confusion around the differentiation of hate crimes from both other crimes *and* from each other (Chakraborti & Garland, 2009). Examining these legislative discrepancies provides insight into their nuanced differences.

Sections 29–32 of the Crime and Disorder Act 1998 outline basic offences that, when motivated by hostility on the grounds of race or religion, become aggravated offences. These include grievous or actual bodily harm; assault and battery; destroying or damaging property; threatening, abusive or insulting conduct toward someone with intent to cause fear of violence or provocation of violence, or cause harassment, alarm or distress; harassment and stalking; and putting people in fear of violence. The aggravating factor can be demonstrated through words, gestures or behaviors, or indicate motivation such as through the victim's affiliation to an identifiable group. These aggravated offences carry higher sentences to recognize the presence of hostility; an assault occasioning actual bodily harm ordinarily has a maximum sentence of 5 years' imprisonment but 7 years if racially or religiously aggravated. Importantly, for accurate data collection, racially and religiously aggravated convictions appear as such on an offender's criminal record and the Police National Database.

Sections 145 and 146 of the Criminal Justice Act 2003 introduced enhanced sentencing in cases motivated by, or involving a demonstration of, hostility toward one of the five protected characteristics. The enhanced penalty cannot exceed the maximum sentence available for the offence, but the Act provides grounds for increasing it within the stipulated range. While this is a matter of judicial discretion, the judge *must* openly state in court the reasons for any sentence enhancement as part of their decision. They do this at the end of the trial, unlike in cases involving aggravated offences that require the prosecution to prove the racial or religious aggravation during the trial. Legislation pertaining to aggravated offences and enhanced sentences are separate. For example, a person charged with the offence of racially aggravated assault may be found not guilty of the racially aggravated part, but instead found guilty of the *basic* offence of common assault; however, the judge cannot increase their sentence using the enhanced sentencing provisions as the charge began as an aggravated offence. Unlike aggravated sentences, data collection in these cases is more difficult as the rationales for sentence enhancements (i.e. motivated by racial hostility) do not appear on offenders' criminal records or the Police National Database.

Finally, the Public Order Act 1986 prohibits a range of conduct that is either intended or likely to stir up hatred on the grounds of race, or is intended to stir up hatred on the grounds of religion or sexual orientation (the penalties for all are the same). Briefly, the conduct covered under this Act includes words and behavior; displaying and distributing written material; public performances and plays; producing or directing programmes; or producing material with a view to it being displayed or shown in a programme. Important differences exist between the nature of the conduct: stirring up *racial* hatred covers threatening, abusive or insulting elements, while stirring up hatred on the basis of religion or sexual orientation *must* be threatening as being abusive or insulting is not enough. This difference, and higher threshold, recognizes the tensions that may emerge because of some faith groups expressing religious or doctrinal opposition to homosexuality, as well as divisions that emerge within or between religious factions. From a harm-reduction perspective, it is pertinent to note that there is no requirement for proof that hatred *was* stirred up; rather, the offences require proof that hatred was *intended* to be stirred up (or *likely to be* in the case of race).

It is evident, therefore, that hate crime laws exist within a punitive paradigm that seeks to impose greater punishments for the prejudice-based element of the offence. While increased punishments do not necessarily prevent crime, they may prove beneficial to the victim or their wider community in other ways. Proponents of hate crime laws claim that increased punishments provide useful *symbolic* gestures to victims and society about the refusal to tolerate certain types of social conduct (Perry & Alvi, 2011). However, these gestures will remain symbolic unless supported by prosecution figures that, according to research, remain significantly low (Walters, Wiedlitzka, Owusu-Bempah, & Goodall, 2017). On the other hand, critics of hate crime laws suggest that they unfairly enhance punitive sanctions for lesser criminalized forms of harm. Jacobs and Potter (1998) were among the first to assert that the enactment of laws designed to address hate (or "bias," as it is often referred to in the United States) indicated more of a political desire to keep the general population happy as opposed to having any real impact on harm reduction or crime prevention. Most crimes, they suggested, comprise of *some* element of hate, prejudice, bias or targeting. Nonetheless, politicians' granting of such legislation generally meant that they would be seen as "doing the right thing" in addressing most victims, harm, crime and bigotry in a seemingly "new" form of legislation.

Variance in Responses to Hate Crime Laws

Subsequent issues to emerge in the hate crime debate include claims of segregation (between regular and hate crimes), homogenization (under the umbrella term of "hate crime"), hierarchization (among different groups), exclusion (from official recognition) and denunciation (being measured against other groups). Carney (2001) offers a more nuanced insight into the development of the hate crime paradigm, indicating that this traditionally involves the targeting of an immutable characteristic; the interchangeability of victims; increased and communal fear within the target group; repeated and/or heightened violence; greater psychological trauma; and victims' reluctance or failure to report victimization. Groups recognized in hate crime statutes have generally been selected based on incurring historical socio-legal persecutions, being over-policed (as offenders) and under-protected (as victims) (Chakraborti & Garland, 2009). These rationales are evident in many groups' lobbying efforts to enact legal protections or offer legal redress for harms incurred because of identity prejudice. As such, considerations of crime victims and their experiences have moved from focusing on the *act* to addressing the victim's *identity*. Demarcating hate crimes in this way is reminiscent of an identity politics approach to policy development (Fraser, 2003). While this has resulted in more targeted approach to prejudice-based victimization, the separate and fixed way in which identity categorization presently works creates a "siloing" effect. The construction of identity hierarchies in this manner both determines outcomes and creates disadvantages:

> [...] hate crime policy has been formed through the work of lobbying and advisory groups who have had quite narrow remits, often focusing exclusively on one area of victimisation. This has contributed to a hierarchy within hate crime policy itself, whereby some identity groups seem to receive preferential treatment in criminal justice responses to hate crime. (Mason-Bish, 2010, p. 62)

These issues were, in part, the focus of the Law Commission's initial exploration into whether hate crime laws in England and Wales required updating and amending. The review assessed (and dismissed) the benefits of extending the Crime and Disorder Act 1998 to include hostility demonstrated toward people on the grounds of disability, sexual orientation or transgender identity, while also examining the case for extending the Public Order Act 1986 to include disability or transgender identity. At that point, the inquiry was not required to consider whether the legislation should apply beyond the five protected characteristics. The ensuing report (Law Commission, 2013, p. 8) proposed the establishment of new Sentencing Council guidelines relating to the five protected characteristics alongside improved recording of data via the Police National Computer. It is evident that the review did not go far enough in its proposals, with the failure to address extending legislation to *new* groups indicative of a lack of awareness of academic scholarship highlighting the exclusionary and discriminatory nature of categorizations among and outside of those selected for an enhanced criminal justice focus.

Schweppe (2012, p. 177) has demonstrated how the recognized hate crime categories in the United Kingdom are minimal compared to some states in the United States that (variously) recognize: citizenship, economic status, family responsibility, matriculation, membership of labor organization, marital status, national origin, personal appearance, political orientation or affiliation, sex and social status. The existence of varied approaches to hate crime inclusion mirrors the subjective status of this particular type of harm. Addressing hate or hostility from a more responsive criminal justice perspective requires dismantling existing, static identity categories that are too exclusive and limiting. This, Schweppe (2012, pp. 182–183) suggests, is a necessary part of efforts to "depoliticise" hate crime:

> [J]uries (or triers of fact) [should] determine whether, on the basis of the evidence before them, a hate crime was committed, rather than curtailing the operation of the legislation to a limited number of (albeit fully deserving) victim groups.

As well as improving inclusivity, this approach may also work in the wider public's favor. Despite several high profile cases, police campaigns and efforts at raising awareness among the public, confusion still exists regarding what constitutes a hate incident or crime and who is protected in law (Duggan & Heap, 2014). A statement released by the Home Office (2013) appeared to include *any* form of hate or hostility, not just that directed to members of a demarcated identity group: "Crimes based on hostility to age, gender, or appearance, for example, can also be hate crimes, although they are not part of the five centrally monitored strands" (p. 11). Following the 2007 murder of Sophie Lancaster murder, the judge drew on the alternative appearance embodied by Sophie and her boyfriend Robert Maltby (who survived the attack) when summing up, describing the act as being a "hate crime" against Goth subculture (Garland, 2010).

Similarly, the Merseyside Police approach to addressing hate crimes toward sex workers demonstrates the flexibility of hate crime policy (Campbell, 2014, 2016, 2018; Corteen, 2018). Campbell (2018, p. 61) argues that "sex workers" experiences fit established definitions foregrounding "othering" and social hierarchies, defining hate crimes as expressions of prejudice, discrimination and power. Vulnerability was central to this application, with sex workers embodying situational vulnerability and minority identity status, therefore, being subject to an enhanced risk of harm. As a result, Campbell's research found that applying the hate crime model to violence against sex workers increased the status of these crimes and the seriousness of reports, improved victim care and dedicated services that monitored investigations and directly investigated some crimes, and led to greater joined-up approaches ensuring safeguarding and justice for sex worker victims of hate crime. While the hate crime approach has not eliminated violence against sex workers in Merseyside, Campbell (2018) argues that "it goes further than many other local regulatory approaches in the UK to prioritize sex worker safety, ensure justice and assert sex workers' equal right to protection" (p. 69).

In hate crime law, reliance on identity categorizations is a double-edged sword. Restricting hate crime to focus on members of minority groups might limit expansion (avoiding a situation whereby *everyone* falls under *some* form of protection, thus, renders the legislation meaninglessness), but selective exclusion may be interpreted by some as a signifier of worthlessness (Hall, 2013). Suggestions of more inclusive approaches to recognizing the types of harm currently addressed by hate crime policies have evolved from reframing the concept as "targeted crime" (Stanko, 2001), through to "targeted vulnerability" (Roulstone & Thomas, 2009) and most recently "vulnerability and difference" (Chakraborti & Garland, 2012). Exploring these, and the potential recourse to human rights law (Schweppe, 2012), Mason (2014, p. 65) suggests that:

> Together, a combination of these approaches may ultimately assist criminal law to rise to the challenge of greater inclusiveness by recognising vulnerability to victimisation based, not necessarily [on] all forms of difference but, rather, on forms of difference that have a claim to equal rights and freedom from unfair or unjustifiable prejudice.

The importance of conceiving of "vulnerability" beyond its traditional understanding has been addressed by Duggan and Heap (2014) who indicate that as well as previously recognizable "risk" factors (such as gender, age or ability), experiencing identity-based hostility, being vulnerable, and being subject to repeat victimization means hate crime victims have commanded a prioritized status in policy formulation. However, complications arise due to the separating out of responses according to different *types* of identity, despite the similarities between these forms of victimization. The potential for duplicated information, inconsistencies in process, blurred boundaries as to what identity categorization might be more suitable (where multiple are present) and general misinformation regarding the action to be taken are some of the pitfalls of having multiple responses available for similar forms of victimization (Duggan & Heap, 2014).

On the other hand, Mason-Bish (2014, p. 31) guards against consolidation, stating that as criminal justice agencies have produced specific guidance for each strand (after consulting with victim groups and campaigners), "a generic hate crime policy might be unwieldy." Either way, encouraging victims to engage with a justice system that may cause them further trauma calls into question the usefulness of enhanced criminalization if this results in victims being be doubly harmed – first by the initial incident, then by the CJS process. Victims of crime are required to engage with the CJS in a co-operative and collaborative manner if they are to avail themselves of the type of (criminal) justice promoted and offered. Hate crimes in particular encompass additional harms and consequences compared to non-targeted forms of victimization (Iganski, 2002). The potential for hate crime victims – particularly those with additional vulnerabilities – to face *secondary* harm because of an unsatisfactory CJS experience may render ineffective any enhancement in perpetrator punishment. Nonetheless, the victim-focused approach of hate crime policy and statute signifies a discernible shift in political policy and the role of the victim in the wider criminal justice system.

THE (RE)EMERGENCE OF VICTIM IDENTITY HIERARCHIES

The surge in UK academic and professional interest in (initially racial) targeted victimization in the late twentieth century was, in part, due to the re-emergence of victimology as an area of scholarly interest and the proliferation of surveys designed to provide data and insight into marginalized and/or vulnerable groups (Bowling, 1999). This, coupled with wider social events linked to racial tensions and criminal justice responses to racial minorities, highlighted the plight of victims in criminal, social and political domains. Deans (2010, p. 199) suggests that dedicated support groups enabled the "extraordinary political reinstatement" of the victim by promoting their political voice and reclaiming spaces while acting on the victim's behalf. Contrastingly, Green (2006, p. 1) has critiqued the turn toward a "victimocracy," underpinned by "the emergence of rule by victim groups" whose demands upon law and policy is tantamount to special treatment:

> [T]oday to be classified as a victim is to be given a special political status, which has no necessary connection with real hardship or actual oppression. Victimhood as a political status is best understood as the outcome of a political strategy by some groups aimed at gaining preferential treatment. In free societies groups often organise to gain advantages for themselves, but the increase in the number and power of groups seeking politically-mandated victim-hood raises some deeper questions.

Victims of crime have not always had access to recognition and redress in criminal justice, although this has been easier for some than others. The socio-political development of the "victim identity" in historical contexts has variously assigned culpability, deservedness and legitimacy to victimhood. Exploring this offers a conceptual framework within which to analyze the discussions around extending hate crime laws to include gender or misogyny given that hate crime studies are a relatively recent development in the victimological field.

Rather than traditionally conceptualized as "innocent" actors in a criminal enterprise, the academic exploration of victimhood was founded on assessing the degree to which the *victim* was culpable for the commission of the criminal act. Three distinct stages characterize academic and political discourse around the victim: their pre-nineteenth century determination as an "essential actor"; their mid-nineteenth to late twentieth century characterization as a "symbolic actor"; and their twentieth century onwards conceptualization as a "fragmented actor" (Kearon & Godfrey, 2007, pp. 30–31). It was due to the scholarly focus during this middle, "symbolic" period that led to the victim occupying a greater role in the central/criminal justice stage, and is of most importance to analyses of hate crime victimization in particular. Key theorists linked to the development of victimology include Benjamin Mendelsohn (1956), Hans von Hentig (1948), Marvin

Wolfgang (1957), Stephen Schafer (1968) and Wolfgang's student Menachem Amir (1971). These early (positivist, male) victimologists sought to investigate the nature of the criminal or victimizing act; the relationship between the criminal and his victim; the actions of either or both preceding the act, and the actions – if any – taken by the victim to deflect or deter the victimization from occurring. Their findings produced several victim typologies which were based on the victim's identity characteristics, their level of responsibility (as indicated by their actions or behaviors), and the degree of attributable victim culpability. These scholars' works set a precedent for what has since been reconceptualized and termed "victim-blaming," with some victims being more adversely affected than others. Victim-blaming discourses first emerged in the 1940s when Mendelsohn identified causal factors that held crime victims to account for the harms they had incurred. His aim was to boost crime prevention efforts using the information he gathered about victim precipitation, facilitation and provocation. Subsequent works by von Hentig, Mendelsohn and Schafer would indicate clear distinctions between identity characteristics and structural factors in terms of victim culpability. Identity aspects, such as the victim's age, gender or mental capacity, may go toward increasing their legitimate claim to victim status, while actions such as provoking a criminal response from an aggressor would lessen or negate this.

The emergence of victim typologies can be seen as linked to, and influential in, developing notions of victim "deservedness" which informs the degree to which victims are seen as more (or less) worthy of justice than others. This in turn can affect access to justice, particularly when coupled with pre-existing stereotypes. The popularity of these early victim typologies influenced further studies on contributory victim precipitation. Wolfgang's (1957) research into homicide indicated that this had often begun with a minor altercation but escalated due to the victim's contributory factors (i.e. carrying weapons, instigating violence or retaliating). However, Wolfgang's student Menachem Amir's research into police reports on forcible rapes in Philadelphia, United States added a new gendered aspect to victim blaming. Using police data, Amir (1971) concluded that a fifth of the rapes in his (limited) sample were victim-precipitated, drawing heavily on prejudicial and sexist ideology when outlining the contributory factors such as the victim being intoxicated, acting or being dressed "seductively," being of dubious reputation or known as sexually "available." The impact of this supposed "expertise" was profound and ongoing; rape and sexual violence continues to be one of the few crimes where the (female) victim's reliability, credibility and potential culpability are scrutinized as closely, if not more so, as those of the alleged perpetrator (Jordan, 2004).

The response from second-wave feminists was to highlight the gendered needs and experiences of female victims, many of whom had been physically or sexually abused by men and faced a significant lack of support services (Cook & Jones, 2007; Hoyle, 2007). The feminist critique exposed implicit bias in measuring victim "deservingness" while simultaneously highlighting the degree to which the "victim" label had become saturated with (masculinist) cultural meaning. They demonstrated how encroaching governance and governmentality was increasingly constructing victims as stakeholders in their own safeguarding (Garland, 1996). This was particularly evident for women held accountable for their own safety and the actions of those who harm them. The qualities associated to different groups of victims according to their identities, experiences or actions and behaviors gives an early indication as to why some groups of victims may be favored over others. The more blameless a victim (or group of victims) appear to be, the easier it is to push punitive law and order policies.

Being at the bottom of any hierarchy may be undesirable, but being omitted altogether means those in most need may have least access to help. People seen by the dominant majority in society to be troublesome or distasteful – for example, rough sleepers, sex workers and those with problematic drug or alcohol dependencies – often find their needs deprioritized. Their marginalization reinforces often-critiqued ideology behind the concept of "victimhood" as encompassing passivity and suffering (Miers, 1978). This imposed passivity is often exacerbated if victims are also considered vulnerable and without autonomy. Butler (2016) guards against disassociating vulnerability and resistance or agency, suggesting that an interrogation of vulnerability may instead result in a greater understanding of agency. Yet while there has been little problematization of mainstream ideologies of passivity and vulnerability afforded to victims of crime, changes have been evident among grassroots circles (Godfrey, Cox, & Farrall, 2007; Newburn & Stanko, 1994) and gendered domains. In particular, criticisms against employing an unproblematized language of vulnerability in relation to gendered victimization have highlighted the wider deleterious effects:

> Our culture, politics, and academic criticism remain troublingly invested in a story of female fragility, a story based on a few key assumptions: women, children and non-masculine men are the victims of male violence, female injury demands society's retribution, and pain renders the victim of violence helpless. (Hagelin, 2013, p. 3)

Feminists' adoption of the term "survivor" to refer to women and children who have survived abuse, most usually from men, is a way of counteracting the disempowering passivity (and elements of culpability) which had come to be associated with the "victim" label (Kelly, 1988; Rock, 2007). Survival is fluid, whereby victimhood appears static or disempowering (Fohring, 2018). Surviving abusive experiences also involves a greater degree of personal investment and struggle to "make it" – something not necessarily captured in victim terminology. As Spalek (2006, p. 26) indicates: "Underpinning the 'victim as survivor' identity is the theme of individual victim as agent who has resisted their abuse to become emotionally and psychologically stronger."

Similar critiques prompted Nils Christie's (1986) seminal work on the "ideal victim," elements of which still permeate popular and political discourses around victims and victimization (Duggan, 2018). Christie noted how legitimate victim status, or deserving victims, were popularly characterized in specific ways. They should be weak in relation to the offender, ideally female, sick, very old or very young. They should be virtuous, or engaged in legitimate, everyday activity, therefore blameless for what happened to them. They should be unrelated to the offender; this "stranger" element also implied that it is a person, not an organization, who committed the (singular) offence. The offender should be big and bad, allowing the victim to elicit unqualified sympathy through their attained victim status. The weak, vulnerable, disempowered victim contrasts the strange, scary and motivated perpetrator in a way that provides a clear dichotomy, or divisions, in numerous respects. Situating victims on binaries both against offenders *and* against one another leads to problematic hierarchies. Victim hierarchies based on the "ideal victim" categorization drew on victims' innate identity character-istics such as gender and age. Christie's (1986) ideal victim concept marries with Aradau's (2004) "politics of pity," whereby emotions toward victims are used by governments to reconstruct and manage their situation, as long as the suffering is recognizable, identifiable and induces sympathy. The nature of the suffering is not necessarily reflective of any inherent value but may feed into responses to it. Exploring who, how and why individuals or groups become worthy of pity, and how this shapes criminal justice responses to them can be illuminating.

As outlined earlier, the current justice approach to hate crimes is one of enhanced punitiveness, with the rationale for additional penalties based on the prejudice harbored by the perpetrator toward the victim(s). Mason (2014, p. 65) outlines the purpose of this, suggesting that "hate crime laws rely upon the mecha-nism of punitive justice to achieve, not just the instrumental goals of retributivist justice, but also the wider symbolic goals of social justice." Therefore, laws have the potential to address socially or politically informed hostilities that can mani-fest as hate crimes. The following section explores the dynamics of gender-based violence and violence against women, examining the contradictions between the-ories of justice and the lived realities of harm to more fully explore the potential for hate crime statutes to address misogyny or gender hostility.

HATE, HOSTILITY AND VIOLENCE AGAINST WOMEN

Violence against women is currently being afforded an unprecedented level of vis-ibility globally, with past, present and potential victims occupying a central role in this rhetoric. Recent events such as the global #MeToo movement has given a platform for many to share their experiences of sexual harassment and vic-timization. A substantial amount of feminist research on gender-based violence (GBV) and violence against women (VAW) has highlighted women's vulnerabil-ity to violent victimization, seemingly based on gender alone. The World Health Organisation and United Nations both estimate that 35% of women worldwide will experience physical and/or sexual violence at some point in their lives (FRA, 2014; United Nations, 2015; WHO, 2013). Similarly, reports indicate that up to 70% of women globally have experienced physical and/or sexual violence from an intimate partner specifically (WHO, 2013). Patriarchy is evident in much of this violence, particularly when it is fatal; most domestic murders of women are by their male partner (Aldridge & Browne, 2003; Howarth, Stimpson, Barran, & Robinson, 2009; Howe & Alaattinoğlu, 2018). Often, the reasons given are indica-tive of male entitlement: threats to his "honour" through her supposed insubor-dination, promiscuity or infidelity; her rejecting him; her requesting a separation and so forth (Dobash, Dobash, & Cavanagh, 2009; Howe, 2018). Family rela-tions can make it difficult for victims to escape abuse, particularly if there is an expectation that women will remain in a relationship or face wider family abuse or condemnation (Gill, 2014). In the United Kingdom, the Forced Marriage Unit provides direct support to hundreds of victims annually, while the United Nations estimate that many thousands of women are victims of family-perpetrated "honour" violence annually across the globe (Manjoo, 2012).

Hate crime victimization research has indicated that gender can be a key feature in the disproportionate targeting of women. Higher levels of vulnerability and risk of harm – particularly sexual harm – are notable among women with disabilities (Casteel, Martin, Smith, Gurkha, & Kupper, 2008; Sherry, 2010). Verbal, physical and sexual threats made by men toward Muslim women who wear religious clothing such as the hijab or niqab illustrate a range of gendered elements, from experiencing the voyeuristic "male gaze" through to expressions of male entitlement to women's bodies (Chakraborti & Zempi, 2012; Zempi & Chakraborti, 2014). In their analysis of women's experiences of street harassment, Mason-Bish and Zempi (2019, p. 12) indicate how the gendered environment of public space is illustrative of structural hierarchies of power where "to be a woman in public is to be available for men's comments." Mason-Bish and Duggan (2019) highlighted similar findings in their empirical research on gendered victimization, with women citing far greater and more frequent experiences of verbal and physical harassment.

Where hostility is directed at women as a group, the fear of violence – especially sexual violence – can lead to women altering their behaviors to reduce perceived risks even if they have not directly experienced harm or threats (Jenness & Broad, 1994). Individual acts of violence against women send a message to *all* women that they should "stay in their place" (Pickup, Williams, & Sweetman, 2001, p. 20). The degree to which acts of violence against individual women can subordinate and frighten women on a wider scale has led feminist scholars to reconceptualize this, initially as "sexual terrorism" (Sheffield, 1992) and more recently as "domestic terrorism" (Pain, 2014). It is notable that the use of this language does not put VAW/GBV on par with discussions around "global terrorism" despite affecting women internationally. The conceptualization as terrorism indicates how the potentiality of this actual or symbolic violence not only serves to regulate women, but also can cause them to internalize fears of victimization to the extent that this has detrimental consequences on their mental health (Silvestri & Crowther-Dowey, 2008; Westbrook, 2008).

In terms of GBV/VAW, there is potential in considering victimization from a perspective of *similarity* rather than difference. Violence against women, as with other forms of recognized hate crime, affect both the individual and their wider community. This is why Carney (2001, p. 319) argues that "rape is the paradigmatic hate crime." Drawing on the immutable characteristic notion of what characterizes hate crimes, she asserts that like other hate crime victims

> the rape victim is selected because she possesses and immutable characteristic – her gender ....
> Rape is not an act of violence that simply happens to women – it is an act of hate that happens
> to women because they are women. (Carney, 2001, pp. 319–320)

The failure to consider rape as a gendered hate crime may reflect the status of law as a traditionally androcentric domain (MacKinnon, 1991). The inherently masculinist nature of legislation (including hate crime laws) makes the consideration of gender or gendered perspectives for inclusion more difficult (Gill & Mason-Bish, 2013). As with much discourse around violence against women, male agency is frequently removed or denied, especially cases of domestic or sexual violence where women are often framed as being manipulative in order for the crimes against them, or perpetrators of harm, to be excused or mitigated (Howe, 2018). The "message" element of hate crimes is further evidence of the power of social regulation through the fear or threat of violence; individual violent acts work to subordinate members of the target group(s) by instilling fear among group members (Westbrook, 2008). As well as focusing on crime prevention, this may also involve dealing with or managing the impact of crime once event has taken place.

While victim policy remains focused on fitting "new" categories of victims into existing moulds, victims' specific needs or wants will remain unmet. With regards hate crime, demarcating along identity lines or arbitrarily enhancing the criminalization of existing offences is unlikely to reduce or prevent targeted victimization. An examination of the social and economic factors *underpinning* such prejudice – perhaps especially that which is gendered – must also be present to effect positive change. To do this requires adequate recognition that people embody multiple (minority) identities, therefore, may be more vulnerable to targeted victimization else victims "fall through gaps":

> Conceiving of hate crimes simply as offences directed towards individual strands of a person's identity fails to give adequate recognition to the interplay of identities with one another and with other personal, social and situational characteristics. (Chakraborti, 2015, p. 17)

The concept of "intersectionality" (Crenshaw, 1989) seeks to remedy this by recognizing and providing space for different sites of identity to meet – or intersect – as parts of a whole. Intersectionality usually refers to the different identities one person will embody (e.g. their race, gender, class, age, etc.) at any given time. This means addressing the different aspects of a person's identity that may have resonance in the victimization they have experienced, or render them more a vulnerable target due to the intersections of race, ethnicity, transgender identity, class and disability (Chakraborti & Zempi, 2012; Meyer, 2008). Research on people's experiences of prejudice on multiple bases has indicated the futility and falsification of trying separate out intent or impact along identity lines (Fogg-Davis, 2006; Lloyd, 2005; Spelman, 1990). Therefore, addressing intersectionality and targeted victimization at policy level may be more effective if focused on harmonizing, rather than separating out, identity-based initiatives (Duggan & Heap, 2014). For women in particular, situating intersectionality alongside gender indicates the complexities of the current hate crime siloing approach and the impact of excluding gender or misogyny as a discreet category. To assess these issues in more depth, the following section explores two case studies: the first addressing the intersectionality of gender and sexual orientation in lesbian women's victimization, and the second outlining how misogyny manifests in the online gender-based victimization of women.

Case Study One: Intersectionalities of Gender and Sexual Identity in Violence Against Women

Violence against women, alongside violence against people who identify as lesbian, gay, bisexual, transgender or queer (**LGBTQ**), is variously acknowledged in domestic and international policy and law. The recognition of a woman's right to be free from gender-based violence has been codified in international human rights, including the *Convention for the Elimination of All Forms of Discrimination Against Women*[1] and the *Declaration on the Elimination of Violence Against Women*.[2] These pre-date the recognition of sexual orientation as requiring specific protection (established in 2011) despite earlier recognition that discrimination based on gender *and* sexual orientation render lesbians more vulnerable to victimization. The Special Rapporteur reports on Torture and Cruel, Inhuman or Degrading Treatment or Punishment noted how perceived deviance from socially constructed gender expectations had resulted in sexual minorities being disproportionately subjected to dehumanization, ill-treatment and torture, with a particular focus on specific allegations of abuses perpetrated against lesbians, including rape and sexual violence, as a means of intimidation and social regulation.[3]

There is a growing acceptance in perceptions of biological sex (i.e. male/female) as being different to gender (i.e. man/woman) with socially constructed gender roles often being measured against a dominant form of heteronormativity (Butler, 1990; Meyer, 2008). These socially imposed gender roles guide the "acceptable" behavior of particular genders, reinforcing compliance or punishing "deviance" with the threat or actuality of hate-based violence. Set against a backdrop of male violence toward women, research has indicated that women are "more likely to be attacked when they [are] not performing gender appropriately" with the added dynamic that the victimization they experience functions as a regulatory tool to others (Mason-Bish, 2014, p. 24). The added dynamic of embodying an LGBTQ identity may exacerbate these perceptions of deviance – and exposure to victimization – along both gender and sexual orientation lines.

This regulatory approach has become increasingly evident alongside greater variations in the way people visibly express and identify their gender (Dragiewicz, 2008; Stearns, 1995). While gender does not determine a person's sexual orientation, the two links in the sense that a person's gender is associated with how others infer their sexual orientation. Additionally, sexual orientation is determined not only by a reading of the individual's gender but also the gender(s) of those in whom they have a sexual interest (Stearns, 1995). In recent years, the socially constructed nature of gender has led to a multiplicity of both gender and sexual orientation identities emerging in line with a greater awareness of variance within these (i.e. non-binary, genderqueer, asexual, pansexual, etc.). However, where specificity remains constant – for example, lesbians being women with a sexual interest in other women – gender and sexual orientation coalesce within the lesbian identity.

Bell and Perry (2015) assert that homosexuality is associated with the violation of gender norms, therefore homophobia is considered to be informed by heterosexism; the promotion of heteronormativity alongside an ideological stigmatization of non-heterosexual behaviors and identities (Herek, 2000). Heteronormativity promotes attraction to the opposite sex, so deviation from this norm simultaneously implies gender role deviation, which can lead to responses rooted in patriarchal fear and hatred. This may be implicit or explicit, given that patriarchy is understood to be "...a system of social structures, and practices in which men dominate, oppress and exploit women" (Walby, 1989, p. 214). Societies shaped by religious doctrine and mandated by male authorities have developed attitudes and systems that promote and normalize male dominance, supposedly on (male) interpretations of doctrine that depict women as inherently inferior or subservient to men. Heteronormative regulation of women's identities, behaviors and expressions embodies the heteropatriarchal notion that women are submissive to men, which in turn emphasizes the heterosexual dynamic of violence against women (Hearn, 1998). This dynamic plays a significant role in hate crimes committed against women generally, and LGBQ women specifically as the interactional dynamics between sexual orientation, gender, and patriarchy creates a toxic environment for those who do not conform to expectations. However, to capture the gendered nature of this victimization, it is more accurate to describe this as "lesbophobia" (Robson, 1992).

VAW and lesbophobia/homophobia share characteristics, such as often taking the form of "low-level" victimization (i.e. verbal abuse, intimidation or threats of physical assault) reported to peers or third parties rather than authorities. These incidents rarely result in victims accessing any form of criminal justice, or even receiving wider public attention. The presence of a sensationalist element can instigate media coverage, particularly if it conforms to popular tropes. An example of this was the voluminous press attention paid to a 2019 incident involving two women attacked on a bus by four teenage boys in London, England. The group verbally harassed the women in a sexually aggressive manner, including demands that they kiss for the boys' entertainment. Upon failing to do so, members of the group physically attacked the women whereupon the image of their bloody and distraught faces quickly gained traction in the press. Several boys in the group were charged with aggravated hate crime offences (BBC News, 2019). As there is no gender or misogyny hate crime strand currently available, and as the women identified as lesbian, pursuing the case as hostility based upon sexual orientation prejudice appears prudent. However, this incident was inherently misogynistic – it was the women's gender *and* their sexual identity that was being centered on in the demands made for the boys' voyeuristic entertainment. Furthermore, it was the women's insubordination to the boys' demands to kiss which resulted in them being subject to male violence; their sexual identities alone were not the initial grounds for hostility. Therefore, the women's gender is crucial to understanding this incident, yet it will be pursued as a homophobic hate crime.

Lesbians who alter their appearance or behaviors in an attempt to "pass" as heterosexual to deter lesbophobic/homophobic victimization from heterosexual men may avoid this, but instead be subjected to sexist or misogynistic abuse due to the relative impunity with which men's verbal hostility toward women is treated (Connell, 1992; Ferraro, 1996; Mason-Bish & Duggan, 2019). Social theorists have noted how societies (and the labels they produce) variously create and reinforce roles and norms through seemingly everyday practices which become embedded to the point of naturalization (Goffman, 1974). Inherent power structures function to construct hegemonic perspectives on identity, which inform social institutions and cultural practices (Connell, 1987). The regularity and familiarity of these structured actions serve to reinforce their naturalization, only becoming evident when imposed "norms" are transgressed in some way (Messerschmidt, 1993). However, rather than demonstrating the multiplicity of ways of being, these transgressions may result in reinforcing the naturalized construction of the pre-existing state of being. Notions of difference, therefore, are assessed along hierarchical lines and benchmarked against this pre-existing state; actions to reinforce, sustain or impose divisions may be read as "doing difference" (Perry, 2001) in that the symbolic nature of targeting based on difference reinforces segregation as natural rather than problematizing it. Men's verbal or physical hostility toward lesbians invokes this hierarchy, initially at the point of expression and subsequently in the absence of social condemnation.

Responses to targeted abuse have sought to capture the wider social dynamics informing prejudice. Drawing on Goffman's idea of "framing," Snow and Benford (1988, 1992) explored the potential of "collective action frames" in providing foundations upon which social campaigns are built. These campaigns are characterized by shared action-oriented beliefs and used to negotiate the wider socio-political environment that embeds and responds to activism. Lesbian (and gay) anti-violence movements have used collective action frames to expose the structural factors informing and sustaining lesbophobic/homophobic prejudice in a given society. However, Jenness and Broad (1994) demonstrated how a gendered analysis did not feature as prominently in these movements as it had in the feminist arena. The failure to recognize the impact of patriarchy in lesbophobic (and homophobic) victimization created a distance between the two movements where a shared approach was needed. Intentionally or otherwise, critiques of patriarchy at the time developed the notion of "sexual terrorism" along heterosexual lines. Sheffield (1992, p. 392) defined sexual terrorism as "a system by which males frighten and, by frightening, dominate and control females" through actual and implied violence. The implied element was of significance as it speaks to the socially controlling potential of fear that serves to regulate behaviors. The notion of sexual terrorism expands on Brownmiller's (1975) work which indicated how men benefited from social control techniques (such as instances of rape) which primarily affected women, even if they were not complicit in manifesting these. Davis (1994) also noted the base level at which such control can operate in public environments, citing street harassment as a means through which to remind women of their vulnerability to sexual violence. The appropriation of the language of terror was more recently adopted by Pain (2014) who argued that within the private sphere, domestic violence can be considered a form of "everyday terrorism."

The wider turn to patriarchy and the framework of structural analysis it offered in highlighting women's victimization at the hands of male perpetrators was fundamental to connect instances of violence across time periods, cultures and societies. Indeed, as Caputi (1992, p. 240, original emphasis) noted, "one of the most significant achievements of the Women's Liberation Movement has been the naming of *sexual violence* as a systematic form of patriarchal oppression." This in turn necessitated a gendering of the subjects (usually women) and objects (usually men) of fear, as well as the types of violence involved. Certainly, many cases of men's violence toward lesbians comprises of a sexualized component that addresses the woman's gender and sexual orientation in a threatening manner. Nonetheless, Jenness and Broad (1994) highlighted the failure to apply this gendered analysis to lesbophobic/homophobic victimization. Examining several US anti-violence campaigns that were either gay and lesbian-sponsored or feminist-inspired, they discovered (at the time) that:

> There is no advice given regarding whether women should report the rape to a gay/lesbian anti-violence project, a feminist-sponsored anti-violence project, or both. Thus, violence against lesbians as *women* is omitted from the work of gay and lesbian-sponsored anti-violence projects. (Jenness & Broad, 1994, p. 414, original emphasis)

This separation continues in societies where hate crime legislation exists. Lesbian women form a minority cohort in both homophobic hate crime *and* violence against women data, research and policy. In foregrounding gender, the VAW literature prioritizes the experiences of "women" but may overlook some of the nuanced aspects affecting lesbian women specifically. On the other hand, in foregrounding sexuality, homophobia scholarship may overlook *women's* experiences specifically when seeking to account for hate and bias based upon sexual orientation prejudice. Therefore, lesbian women's intersectional experiences may be sidelined or omitted on the basis of both gendered and sexuality differences by virtue of not being dominant in either domain, but do feature in hate crime paradigms. By comparison, violence against heterosexual women – who do not occupy a recognized protected characteristic – does not enter the hate crime framework of analysis based on gender alone.

Case Study Two: Misogyny in the Online Gender-based Victimization of Women

The advent and proliferation of social media is a key element of social change that features heavily in contemporary experiences of gendered or misogynistic victimization (KhosravikNik & Esposito, 2018). Social media facilitates greater interactions between people in virtual spaces, with free-to-use platforms *Facebook*, *Instagram* and *Twitter* dominating among the most popular forums where people can indulge their desire for "constant connectivity" (Keipi, Nasi, Oksanen, & Rasanen, 2017, p. 2). Since its creation in 2006, *Twitter* in particular has become an immensely prevalent means of sharing information and comment globally. However, alongside the rise in popularity of social media has been a proliferation of harmful and problematic behaviors leading to the development of a "new frontier for spreading hate" (Banks, 2010, p. 234). Hardaker (2013) outlines how the "trolling" of individuals involves targeting them for abuse and harassment, usually by unidentifiable people, in a manner that can escalate very quickly in a largely unregulated cyberspace. The use of this term for online misogyny specifically has been critiqued on the basis that it "does not adequately capture the sexually explicit rhetoric, stark misogyny, or violence of contemporary gendered cyberhate" (Jane, 2017, p. 65). Instead, Jane (2017, p. 64) offers an overview of how these behaviors have also been variously described as "cyber harassment" (Citron, 2014), "technology violence" (Ostini & Hopkins, 2015), "technology-facilitated sexual violence" (Henry & Powell, 2015, 2018), "gendertrolling" (Mantilla, 2015), "cyber VAWG" (United Nations, 2015) and "cybersexism" (Poland, 2016).

The proliferation of terms addressing the gendered nature of online abuse has emerged in tandem with research on the issue. A UN report (2015) which evidenced the significantly gendered nature of online hostility detailed how almost three-quarters (73%) of women and girls had experienced or been exposed some form of online violence, with those at heightened risk being aged between 18 and 24 years old. Organized forms of this "cybersexism" involves men using technology to express their vilification of, and power over, women (Poland, 2016, p. 3). In the gaming world, the online abuse of high-profile women became prolific enough to be termed #Gamergate (Braithwaite, 2018). In the United Kingdom, women with high profiles have been targeted, including Cambridge Professor Mary Beard (who received bomb threats following a television appearance), Caroline Criado-Perez (who received rape and death threats for her campaign to have Jane Austen represented on a sterling bank note) and Labor MP Stella Creasy (who received rape threats for publicly supporting Criado-Perez's campaign) (Hardaker & McGlashan, 2016, "Real men don't hate women": Twitter rape threats and group identity). While two of Criado-Perez's abusers – Isabella Sorley and John Nimmo – were jailed for several weeks, for the most part misogynistic abuse remains unchallenged or unreported on *Twitter*.

The rise in "technology-facilitated sexual violence" (Henry & Powell, 2015, Embodied harms: Gender, shame, and technology-facilitated sexual violence) goes far beyond harassment, encompassing threats, image-based abuse, cyberstalking, impersonation and a phenomenon directly linked to the cyber domain: doxing. Doxing, or disseminating someone's personal information online without their consent, incites Internet antagonists or encourage and enable people to "hunt targets offline" (Jane, 2017, p. 68). However, the futility of policing the vast number of sexist, misogynistic or threatening comments made to online women commentators means tolerance levels of certain types of online abuse alter accordingly to the point where such behavior is expected or even anticipated (Moynihan, 1993). Bannister and Kearns (2009, p. 182) have indicated how

> the sociospatial situation in which we find ourselves both influences our predisposition towards tolerance and determines a set of other drivers of the tolerant response, so that our thresholds of tolerance are spatially specific and spatially variant.

Consequently, some types of behavior – or some types of victim – may become acceptable in settings where levels of tolerance and behavioral expectations fuel, lessen or fundamentally alter perceptions of "legitimate" victimization.

The anonymity afforded to users breeds otherwise morally objectionable behaviors that inform enhanced notions of disinhibition and de-individuation (KhosravikNik & Esposito, 2018). Trolling on *Twitter* has provided ample evidence of the "normalising of deviancy," where ordinary people are increasingly guilty of new forms of deviance in comparison to traditionally deviant criminal behaviors, which are increasingly seen as normal (Krauthammer, 1993, p. 20). What may begin with isolated commentators can quickly become groups of people actively harassing a particular target. Therefore, linked to de-individuation is the rise in group salience and polarization, often achieved by bringing previously diverse individuals or fragmented groups together through fostering "a collective identity and sense of community" (Banks, 2010, p. 234). These communities engage in prejudice enacted through "hate speech"; hatred is expressed against particular targets while they are simultaneously excluded from

> participating in the broader deliberative processes required for democracy to happen, by rendering them unworthy of participation and limiting the likelihood of others recognising them as legitimate participants in speech. (Gelber, 2011, p. 198)

Hate speech can incite physical violence. Williams' (2006) research demonstrated the virtual and physical offending patterns of perpetrators of online misogyny. This is evident through the rise of online groups of men who identify as "involuntary celibates," otherwise known as "incels." Incels are an increasingly global phenomenon whose actions and beliefs are reminiscent of patriarchal ideologies imbued with misogynistic values. Online communities of incels are mainly composed of men who share the collective experience of being denied sex by women; this "inceldom" is characterized as incredibly self-loathing and aggressive toward anybody who is sexually active (Williams, 2018). Occupying areas of the internet commonly referred to as the "manosphere," incels upload blogs, forums and podcasts linked to men's rights activism, regularly decrying feminists and women's groups by using misogynist language and imagery (Marwick & Caplan, 2018). Members seek encouragement and justification through engaging in online discussions through social media platforms; sometimes implicated in attacks labeled as "gender terrorism" by the mass media (Squirrell, 2018). The activities demonstrated by members of these groups illustrate the inherent dangers of involuntary celibacy ideology within a wider misogynistic online sphere. This includes vitriolic backlashes against supposed "feminist agendas" and anti-rape efforts, with many claiming that rape culture is little more than a feminist-inspired moral panic (Gotell & Dutton, 2016). Marwick and Caplan (2018, p. 70) demonstrate how men's rights activists rely on adverse feminist reactions, often manipulating academic work to reinforce and justify their claims to deluded feminist agendas. The largely unrestricted nature of the Internet means that the misogynistic language and toxic views about women that are central to the involuntary celibate agenda may encourage individuals to commit violent crimes in the real world.

Incel group dynamics allow for a collective loss of individuality and, in turn, personal responsibility for activities otherwise deemed morally abhorrent. The growth of shared ideologies leads to the formation of cyber "mobs" (Citron, 2009) whose identities are often polarized from those they seek to denigrate. The expression of strong, inflammatory and often controversial opinions are designed to attract the attention (and support) of likeminded others, and are more easily fostered in an online – as opposed to physical – environment. Known as "flaming," members' engagement in such behaviors help reinforce the collective identity uniting affiliates while also setting up the context in which "martyrs" – those who act out their hatred – emerge. Jane (2017) has indicated how the evolution of such "flaming" behaviors when targeted at women specifically highlight the inherent misogyny that has come to shape the collective targeting of women while also raising the profile of men affiliated to such abusive rhetoric.

The 2014 Isla Vista Killings and the 2018 Toronto Van Attack indicate the potential power of these cyber-dynamics. In Isla Vista, 22-year-old Elliot Rodger uploaded an autobiographical manifesto and YouTube video where he outlined his misery, loneliness and aggression, blaming women for him still being a virgin; soon after, he killed six people and injured a further fourteen before shooting himself. Incels who considered Rodger a martyr for the cause and a hero lauded him online. Among them was Toronto resident Alek Minassian, who posted a Facebook status praising Elliot Rodger: "The Incel Rebellion has already begun! We will overthrow all the Chads and Stacys! All Hail the Supreme Gentleman Elliot Rodger!" (BBC News, 2018). Moments later, Minassian drove a large van into members of the public, killing 10 people and injured 14 more. As before, several online posts surfaced praising Minassan as a community hero and thanking him for his service to the "cause." Such evident male entitlement indicates a correlation between patriarchal ideals of rights and expectations, particularly around women's bodies and sexuality; this is espoused by Incel ideology that in turn justifies gendered acts of aggression and violence (DeKeseredy & Schwartz, 2016).

The power of virtual condemnation becomes more powerful as global connectivity increases. With this comes the potential for the enhanced persecution of those accessing such spaces. KhosraviNik and Esposito (2018, p. 55) suggest that while academic insight into cyberhate has evolved rapidly:

> gender has not received sufficient institutional and academic attention as a source of hate in its own right. While the dangers and risks of the digital world are well acknowledged, we still lack a clear grasp of what it actually entails being a woman navigating the cyberspace, and which specific threats and troubles this journal can bring about.

In their research into victims of online misogyny, Lewis, Rowe, and Wiper (2018, p. 528) indicated how discerning actual hatred was difficult as "perpetrators seemed not to hate women in a categorical sense but rather to be motivated by a perception that women engaging in feminist debate were transgressing appropriate gender roles." In other words, it is a powerful, cheap and almost effortless way to silence, control and contain women in virtual spaces. Similarly, D'Souza, Griffin, Schackleton, and Walt (2018) explored the failure to legislate against gender hate speech in Australia, showing how the nature and impact of this speech, alongside the direct and indirect harms affiliated to this form of victimization, highlighted the silencing impact gender hate speech can have on all women – not just those directly targeted by such hostility. They argue that regulating gender hate speech is necessary to enhance women's agency, particularly in the public domain, allowing them equal access to civil society.

The open nature of such spaces and wider visibility to others beyond the intended targets means the impact can be much wider ranging. Weinstein (1992) categorized the collective fear of a victim's cultural group following the victimization of members of that group as the "in terrorem" effect to demonstrate how wide the impacts of harm can resonate. Jenness and Grattet (2001, p. 179) argue that states have a responsibility to ensure the safety and security of vulnerable groups in a way that affirms "prosocial values of tolerance and respect" to wider society. The enactment of laws against such harm sends an important message that liberal democracies have a "strong interest … in promoting diversity and demonstrating equal concern and respect for all citizens" (Al-Hakim & Dimock, 2012, p. 572). The failure to fully implement such laws and safety practices may be rooted in structural notions of victim-blaming directed toward women targets of gendered cyberhate; instead of support and assistance, they incur further shame and blame in a manner reminiscent of traditional forms of domestic, sexual and gendered victimization prevention "advice":

> Advising or coercing women to opt out of or dramatically change their online engagement is a form of digital disenfranchisement. It is at odds with the recognition by an increasing number of nations that equality of access to affordable and effective broadband is vital for nations' economic and social development. (Jane, 2017, p. 73)

In line with traditional approaches to gendered victimization, directing the (female) cyber victim to modify, limit or forgo their online presence is an easier and more convenient activity than seeking out or reprimanding the (male) cyber perpetrator.

CONCLUSION

The exclusion of gender or misogyny from hate crime protections in England and Wales has been founded on several grounds: women not constituting a "minority," the presumption that much of the victimization they experience takes place within the context of an interpersonal or familial relationship, and the fact that legislative protections already exist to address many of these harms (Mason-Bish, 2014). It is true that not *all* violence against women is rooted in hate or hostility, but the invoking of such thresholds for debates on gender and misogyny hate crime (but not other strands) is telling. Much gender-based victimization which involves repeat or targeted elements – for example, online hostility – would likely be characterized as "more serious" in nature if considered a hate crime. This in turn would require more active protections and responses by organizations and statutory agencies. The continued failure to include gender or misogyny is testament to the gendered power structures in society that determine which gender dictates the law. Linked to this is the knowledge that, traditionally, engagement with the criminal justice system has not been a positive experience for women as victims of crime and may account for why many women remain silent about the harms they have incurred. Therefore, if the law was changed to incorporate gender or misogyny as recognized grounds of hostility for the purposes of prosecution, whether or not women would avail themselves of this legal redress remains to be seen.

Those active as advocates, practitioners or campaigners in the field of violence against women prevention have also expressed caution about the ability of hate crime policy as it currently stands to address issues of intersectionality and diversity in gendered harm at a sophisticated level (Gill & Mason-Bish, 2013). While it is encouraging that the Law Commission are looking at this issue again in light of ongoing cultural developments (i.e. #metoo), it is important to note that legislation which targets individuals and acts can only do so much; real change needs to come at a structural level. The prevalence of violence against women is the result of unequal power relations between men and women in society (Pickup, Williams, & Sweetman, 2001). Many forms of male violence against women are reminiscent of existing hate crimes in terms of intent, approach and impact, yet the issue may not be with the *gender* of the victim per se but the gender relations informing the aggressor's feelings of entitlement and resentment toward the victim. This is why it is important to include in protections as it fits with the framework used for other characteristics. However, it is important to acknowledge that addressing gender or misogyny in hate crime legislation may do much for data collection and capture, but likely very little to effectively reduce actual victimization.

In terms of whether it should be "gender" or "misogyny" that is recognized, valid arguments exist for both. While adopting "misogyny" would highlight the specificity of this type of abuse and who is affected, it risks being considered exclusionary (of men) and potentially underused if the term is one that people are unfamiliar with or misunderstand. Adopting "gender" not only lends itself to greater inclusivity but also allows for people of all genders (and none) to avail themselves of these protections. In doing so, scholars, practitioners and policymakers will be able to clearly see the differences between who is (and is not) experiences or reporting gender hate crime, who/what this involves and what – if any – criminal justice outcomes arise as a result. This is vital if efforts to recognize, respond and reduce targeted victimization on the basis of gender are to prevail.

NOTES

1. G.A. Res. 34/180, UN GAOR Supp. No. 46.
2. G.A. Res. 48/04, 48 UN GAOR Supp. No. 49.
3. UN Doc. A/56/156, July 3, 2001 and UN Doc. E/CN.4/2002/76, December 27, 2001.

REFERENCES

Aldridge, M. L., & Browne, K. D. (2003). Perpetrators of spousal homicide: A review. *Trauma, Violence & Abuse, 4*(3), 265–276.

Al-Hakim, M., & Dimock, S. (2012). Hate as an aggravating factor in sentencing. *Criminal Law Review, 15,* 572–611.

Amir, M. (1971). *Patterns of forcible rape*. Chicago, IL: University of Chicago Press.

Aradau, C. (2004). The perverse politics of four-letter words: Risk and pity in the securitisation of human trafficking. *Millennium – Journal of International Studies, 33*(2), 251–278.

Banks, J. (2010). Regulating hate speech online. *International Review of Law, Computers and Technology, 24*(3), 233–239.

Bannister, J., & Kearns, A. (2009). Tolerance, respect and civility amid changing cities. In A. Millie (Ed.), *Securing respect: Behavioural expectations and anti-social behaviour in the UK*. Bristol: Policy Press.

BBC News. (2018). Elliot Roger: How misogynist killer became 'incel hero'. Retrieved from https://www.bbc.co.uk/news/world-us-canada-43892189. Accessed on October 10, 2019.

BBC News. (2019, July 25). Homophobic night bus attack: Four teens charged. Retrieved from https://www.bbc.co.uk/news/uk-england-london-49119947

Bell, J., & Perry, B. (2015). Outside looking in: The community impacts of anti-lesbian, gay, and bisexual hate crime. *Journal of Homosexuality, 62*(1), 98–120.

Bowling, B. (1999). *Violent racism, victimisation, policing and social context*. New York, NY: Oxford University Press.

Braithwaite, A. (2018). It's about ethics in games journalism? Gamergaters and geek masculinity. *Social Media + Society*, October–December, 1–10.

Brownmiller, S. (1975). *Against our will: Men, women and rape*. New York, NY: Simon and Schuster.

Butler, J. (1990). *Gender trouble: Feminism and the subversion of identity*. New York, NY: Routledge.

Butler, J. (2016). Rethinking vulnerability and resistance. In J. Butler, Z. Gambetti, & L. Sabsay (Eds.), *Vulnerability in resistance* (pp. 12–27). Durham, NC: Duke University Press.

Campbell, R. (2014). Not getting away with it: Linking sex work and hate crime in Merseyside. In N. Chakraborti & J. Garland (Eds.), *Responding to hate crime: The case for connecting policy and research* (pp. 55–70). Bristol: Policy Press.

Campbell, R. (2016). *Not getting away with it: Addressing violence against sex workers as hate crime in Merseyside*. Durham, NC: University of Durham.

Campbell, R. (2018). Beyond hate: Policing sex work, protection and hate crime. In T. Sanders & M. Laing (Eds.), *Policing the sex industry: Protection, paternalism and politics*. Abingdon: Routledge.

Campbell, R., & Stoops, M. (2010). Taking sex workers seriously: Treating violence as hate crime in Liverpool. *Research for Sex Work*, *12*, 9–12.

Caputi, J. (1992). To acknowledge and heal: 20 years of feminist thought and activism. In C. Kramarae & D. Spender (Eds.), *The knowledge explosion: Generations of feminist scholarship* (pp. 340–352). New York, NY: Teachers College Press.

Carney, K. (2001). Rape: The paradigmatic hate crime. *St John's Law Review*, *75*(2), 315–356.

Casteel, C., Martin, S., Smith, J., Gurkha, K., & Kupper, L. (2008). National study of physical and sexual assault among women with disabilities. *Injury Prevention*, *14*, 87–90.

Chakraborti, N. (2015). Re-thinking hate crime: Fresh challenges for policy and practice. *Journal of Interpersonal Violence*, *30*(10), 1738–1754.

Chakraborti, N., & Garland, J. (2009). *Hate crime: Impact, causes and responses* (1st ed.). London: Sage.

Chakraborti, N., & Garland, J. (2012). Reconceptualizing hate crime victimization through the lens of vulnerability and "difference". *Theoretical Criminology*, *16*(4), 499–514.

Chakraborti, N., & Zempi, I. (2012). The veil under attack: Gendered dimensions of Islamophobic victimisation. *International Review of Victimology*, *18*(3), 269–284.

Christie, N. (1986). The ideal victim. In E. Fattah (Ed.), *From crime policy to victim policy* (pp. 17–30). Basingstoke: Macmillan.

Citron, D. (2009). Law's expressive value in combating cyber gender harassment. *Michigan Law Review*, *108*, 373–418.

Citron, D. (2014). *Hate crimes in cyberspace*. London: Harvard University Press.

Connell, R. (1987). *Gender and power: Society, the person, and sexual politics*. Stanford, CA: Stanford University Press.

Connell, R. (1992). A very straight gay: Masculinity, homosexual experience and the dynamics of gender. *American Sociological Review*, *57*(6), 735–751.

Connell, R. (2007). The northern theory of globalization. *Sociological Theory*, *25*(4), 368–385.

Cook, K., & Jones, H. (2007). Surviving victimhood: The impact of feminist campaigns. In S. Walklate (Ed.), *The handbook of victims and victimology* (pp. 125–145). Bristol: Policy Press.

Corteen, K. (2018). New victimisations: Female sex worker hate crime and the 'ideal victim'. In M. Duggan (Ed.), *Revisiting the 'ideal victim': Developments in critical victimology*. Bristol: Policy Press.

Crenshaw, K. (1989). Demarginalizing the intersection of race and sex: A black feminist critique of antidiscrimination doctrine, feminist theory and antiracist politics. *University of Chicago Legal Forum*, *140*, 139–167.

Davis, D. (1994). The harm that has no name: Street harassment, embodiment, and African American women. *UCLA Women's Law Review*, *4*, 133–178.

Deans, M. (2010). *Governmentality: Power and rule in modern society*. London: Sage.

DeKeseredy, W., & Schwartz, M. (2016). Thinking sociologically about image-based sexual abuse. *Sexualization, Media & Society*, *2*(4), 1–8.

Dobash, R., Dobash, R., & Cavanagh, K. (2009). "Out of the blue": Men who murder an intimate partner. *Feminist Criminology*, *4*(3), 194–225.

Dragiewicz, M. (2008). Patriarchy reasserted: Fathers' rights and anti-VAWA activism. *Feminist Criminology, 4*(3), 194–225.

D'Souza, T., Griffin, L., Schackleton, N., & Walt, D. (2018). Harming women with words: The failure of Australian law to prohibit hate speech. *UNSW Law Journal, 41*(3), 939–976.

Duggan, M. (2013). Working with victims: Values and validations. In M. Cowburn, M. Duggan, A. Robinson, & P. Senior (Eds.), *The values of criminology and community justice* (pp. 239–254). Bristol: Policy Press.

Duggan, M. (2014). Working with lesbian, gay, bisexual and transgender communities to shape hate crime policy. In N. Chakraborti & J. Garland (Eds.), *Responding to hate crime: The case for connecting policy and research* (pp. 87–97). Bristol: Policy Press.

Duggan, M. (2018). Introduction. In M. Duggan (Ed.), *Revisiting the 'Ideal Victim': Developments in critical victimology*. Bristol: Policy Press.

Duggan, M., & Heap, V. (2014). *Administrating victimization: The politics of anti-social behaviour and hate crime policy*. London: Palgrave Macmillan.

Ferraro, K. (1996). Women's fear of victimization: Shadow of sexual assault? *Social Forces, 75*(2), 667–690.

Fogg-Davis, H. (2006). Theorising black lesbians with black feminism: A critique of same-race street harassment. *Politics & Gender, 2*, 57–76.

Fohring, S. (2018). Revisiting the non-ideal victim. In M. Duggan (Ed.), *Revisiting the 'Ideal Victim': Developments in critical victimology*. Bristol: Policy Press.

FRA. (2014). *Violence against women: An EU-Wide Survey*. Vienna: Fundamental Rights Agency.

Fraser, N. (2003). Rethinking recognition: Overcoming displacement and reification in cultural politics. In B. Hobson (Ed.), *Recognition struggles and social movements: Contested identities, agency and power* (pp. 21–34). Cambridge: Cambridge University Press.

Garland, D. (1996). The limits of the sovereign state: Strategies of crime control in contemporary society. *British Journal of Criminology, 36*(4), 445–471.

Garland, J. (2010). "It's a mosher just been banged for no reason": Assessing the victimisation of Goths and the boundaries of hate crime. *International Review of Victimology, 18*(1), 25–57.

Gelber, K. (2011). *Speech matters: Getting free speech right*. Queensland: University of Queensland Press.

Gerstenfeld, P. (2011). *Hate crimes*. London: Sage.

Gill, A., & Mason-Bish, H. (2013). Addressing violence against women as a form of hate crime. *Feminist Review, 105*, 1–20.

Godfrey, B., Cox, D., & Farrall, S. (2007). *Criminal lives: Family life, employment and offending*. Oxford: Oxford University Press.

Goffman, E. (1974). *Frame analysis: An essay on the organization of experience*. Cambridge, MA: Harvard University Press.

Gotell, L., & Dutton, E. (2016). Sexual violence in the 'manosphere': Antifeminist men's rights discourses on rape. *International Journal for Crime, Justice and Social Democracy, 5*(2), 65–80.

Green, D. (2006). *We're (Nearly) all victims now! How political correctness is undermining our liberal culture*. London: Civitas: Institute for the Study of Civil Society.

Hagelin, S. (2013). *Reel vulnerability: Power, pain, and gender in contemporary American film and television*. New York, NY: Rutgers University Press.

Hall, N. (2013). *Hate crime*. Cullompton: Willan.

Hardaker, C. (2013). "Uh....not to be nitpicky,,,,,but...the past tense of drag is dragged, not drug": An overview of trolling strategies. *Journal of Language Aggression and Conflict, 1*(1), 57–85.

Hardaker, C., & McGlashan, M. (2016). "Real men don't hate women": Twitter rape threats and group identity. *Journal of Pragmatics, 91*, 80–93.

Hearn, J. (1998). *The violences of men: How men talk about and how agencies respond to men's violence to women*. London: Sage.

Henry, N., & Powell, A. (2015). Embodied harms: Gender, shame, and technology-facilitated sexual violence. *Violence Against Women, 21*(6), 758–779.

Henry, N., & Powell, A. (2018). Technology-facilitated sexual violence: A literature review of empirical research. *Trauma, Violence & Abuse, 19*(2), 195–208.

Herek, G. (2000). The psychology of sexual preference. *Current Directions in Psychological Science, 9*(1), 12–22.

Home Office. (2013). *Domestic violence disclosure scheme (DVDS) pilot assessment*. London: Home Office.

Howarth, E., Stimpson, L., Barran, D., & Robinson, A. (2009). *Safety in numbers: A multi-site evaluation of independent domestic violence services*. London: Sigrid Rausing Trust/The Henry Smith Charity.

Howe, A. (2008) *Sex, violence and crime: Foucault and the 'man' question*. London: Routledge-Cavendish.

Howe, A., & Alaattinoğlu, D. (2018). *Contesting femicide: Feminism and the power of law revisited*. London: Routledge.

Hoyle, C. (2007). Feminism, victimology and domestic violence. In S. Walklate (Ed.), *The handbook of victims and victimology* (pp. 146–174). Cullompton: Willan.

Iganski, P. (2002). *Hate crimes hurt more, but should they be more harshly punished? The Hate Debate*. London: Profile.

Jacobs, J., & Potter, K. (1998). *Hate crimes: Criminal law and identity politics*. New York, NY: Open University Press.

Jane, E. (2017). Gendered cyberhate, victim-blaming, and why the internet is more like driving a car on a road than being naked in the snow. In E. Martellozzo & E. Jane (Eds.), *Cybercrime and its victims* (pp. 61–78). London: Routledge.

Jenness, V., & Broad, K. (1994). Antiviolence activism and the (in)visibility of gender in the gay/lesbian and women's movement. *Gender & Society, 8*(3), 402–423.

Jenness, V., & Grattet, R. (2001). *Making hate a crime – From social movement to law enforcement*. New York, NY: Russell Sage.

Jordan, J. (2004). Beyond belief? Police, rape and women's credibility. *Criminology & Criminal Justice, 4*(1), 29–59.

Kearon, T., & Godfrey, B. (2007). Setting the scene: A question of history. In S. Walklate (Ed.), *The handbook of victims and victimology* (pp. 17–36). Cullompton: Willan.

Keipi, T., Nasi, M., Oksanen, A., & Rasanen, P. (2017). *Online hate and harmful content: Cross-national perspectives*. London: Routledge.

Kelly, L. (1988). *Surviving sexual violence*. Minneapolis, MN: University of Minnesota Press.

KhosravikNik, M., & Esposito, E. (2018). Online hate, digital discourse and critique: Exploring digitally-mediated discursive practices of gender-based hostility. *Lodz Papers in Pramgatics, 14*(1), 45–68.

Krauthammer, C. (1993). Defining deviancy up. *The New Republic*, pp. 20–25.

Law Commission. (2013). *Consultation Paper 213 – Hate crime: The case for extending the existing offences*. London: Crown.

Lewis, R., Rowe, M., & Wiper, C. (2018). Misogyny online: Extending the boundaries of hate crime. *Journal of Gender-based Violence, 2*(3), 519–536.

Lloyd, M. (2005). *Beyond identity politics: Feminism, power and politics*. London: Sage.

Lyons, C. (2006). Stigma or sympathy? Attributions of fault to hate crime victims and offenders. *Social Psychology Quarterly, 69*(1), 39–59.

MacKinnon, C. (1991). Reflections on sex equality under law. *Yale Law Journal, 100*(5), 1281–1328.

Manjoo, R. (2012). *Report of the special rapporteur on violence against women, its causes and consequences*. United Nations General Assembly.

Manne, K. (2017). *Down girl: The logic of misogyny*. London: Penguin.

Mantilla, K. (2015). *Gendertrolling: How misogyny went viral*. Santa Barbara, CA, Denver, CO: Praeger.

Marwick, A., & Caplan, R. (2018). Drinking male tears: Language, the manosphere, and networked harassment. *Feminist Media Studies, 18*(4), 543–559.

Mason-Bish, H. (2010). Future challenges for hate crime policy: Lessons from the past. In N. Chakraborti & J. Garland (Eds.), *Hate crime: Concepts, policies, future directions* (pp. 169–182). Cullompton: Willan.

Mason, G. (2014) The symbolic purpose of hate crime law: Ideal victims and emotion. *Theoretical Criminology, 18*(1), 75–92.

Mason-Bish, H. (2014). Beyond the silo: Rethinking hate crime and intersectionality. In N. Hall (Ed.), *The Routledge international handbook on hate crime*. London: Routledge.

Mason-Bish, H., & Duggan, M. (2019). "Some men deeply hate women, and express that hatred freely": Examining victims' experiences and perceptions of gendered hate crime. *International Review of Victimology, 23*, 17–32.

Mason-Bish, H., & Zempi, I. (2019). Misogyny, racism and Islamophobia: Street harassment at the intersections. *Feminist Criminology, 14*(5), 540–559.

Mendelsohn, B. (1956). A new branch of bio-psychosocial science: La victimology, *Review International de Criminologie et de Police Technique, 2.*

Messerschmidt, J. (1993). *Masculinities and crime.* Lanham, MD: Rowman & Littlefield.

Meyer, D. (2008). Interpreting and experiencing anti-queer violence: Race, class and gender differences among LGBT hate crime victims. *Race, Gender & Class, 15*(3/4), 262–282.

Miers, D. (1978). *The politicisation of the victim.* Abingdon: Professional Books.

Moynihan, D. (1993). Defining deviancy down. *American Scholar, 62,* 17–30.

Mullany, L., & Trickett, L. (2018). *Misogyny hate crime evaluation report.* Nottingham: Nottingham Women's Centre.

Newburn, T., & Stanko, E. (1994). *Just boys doing business? Men, masculinities and crime.* London: Psychology Press.

Nottingham Citizens. (2014). *No place for hate.* Research report. Retrieved from https://www.nottingham.ac.uk/~lgzwww/contacts/staffPages/stephenlegg/documents/14.10.A-CITIZENS-COMMISSION-NO-PLACE-FOR-HATE.pdf

ODIHR. (2009). *Hate crime laws: A practical guide.* Warsaw: OSCE Office for Democratic Institutions and Human Rights.

Ostini, J., & Hopkins, S. (2015). Online harassment is a form of violence. *The Conversation.* Retrieved from https://theconversation.com/online-harassment-is-a-form-of-violence-38846. Accessed on October 10, 2019.

Pain, R. (2014). Everyday terrorism. *Progress in Human Geography, 38*(4), 531–550.

Perry, B. (2001). *In the name of hate: Understanding hate crime.* New York, NY: Routledge.

Perry, B., & Alvi, S. (2011). 'We are all vulnerable': The in terrorem effects of hate crimes. *International Review of Victimology, 18*(1), 57–71.

Pickup, F., Williams, S., & Sweetman, C. (2001). Explaining violence against women as a developmental concern. In F. Pickup, S. Williams, & C. Sweetman (Eds.), *Ending violence against women: A challenge for development and humanitarian work* (pp. 11–45). Oxford: Oxford University Press.

Poland, B. (2016). *Haters: Harassment, abuse and violence online.* Lincoln, NE: University of Nebraska Press.

Robson, R. (1992). *Lesbian Outlaw: Survival under the rule of law.* University of Michigan, MI: Firebrand Books.

Rock, P. (2007). Theoretical perspectives on victimisation. In S. Walklate (Ed.), *Handbook of victims and victimology* (pp. 37–61). Cullompton: Willan.

Roulstone, A., & Thomas, P. (2009). *Hate crime and disabled people.* Manchester: Equality and Human Rights Commission and Breakthrough UK.

Schafer, S. (1968). *The victim and his criminal: A study in functional responsibility.* New York, NY: Random House.

Schweppe, J. (2012). Defining characteristics and politicising victims: A legal perspective. *Journal of Hate Studies, 10*(1), 173–198.

Sheffield, C. (1992). Hate violence. In P. Rothenberg (Ed.), *Race, class and gender in the United States* (pp. 432–441). New York, NY: St Martin's.

Sherry, M. (2010). *Disability hate crimes: Does anybody really hate disabled people?* Farnham: Ashgate.

Silvestri, M., & Crowther-Dowey, C. (2008). *Gender and crime.* London: Sage.

Snow, D., & Bedford, R. (1988). Ideology, frame resistance, and participant mobilization. *International Social Movement Research, 1*(1), 197–217.

Snow, D., & Bedford, R. (1992). Master frames and cycles of protest. In A. Morris & C. McClurg (Eds.), *Frontiers in social movement theory* (pp. 133–154). New Haven, CT: Yale University Press.

Spalek, B. (2006). *Crime victims: Theory, policy, practice.* Basingstoke: Macmillan.

Spelman, E. (1990). *Inessential woman: Problems of exclusion in feminist thought.* London: The Women's Press.

Squirrell, T. (2018). Don't make the mistake of thinking incels are men's rights activists – They are so much more dangerous. *The Independent,* April 26. Retrieved from https://www.independent.co.uk/voices/incels-alek-minassian-mra-mens-rights-terrorism-toronto-van-attack-a8323166.html. Accessed on October 10, 2019.

Stanko, E. (2001). Re-conceptualising the policing of hatred: Confessions and worrying dilemmas of a consultant. *Law and Critique*, *12*, 309–329.

Stearns, D. (1995). Gendered sexuality: The privileging of sex and gender in sexual orientation. *NWSA Journal*, *7*(1), 8–29.

United Nations. (2015). *Cyber violence against women and girls: A world-wide wake-up call*. UN Broadband Commission for Digital Development Working Group on Broadband and Gender. Retrieved from https://www.unwomen.org/~/media/headquarters/attachments/sections/library/publications/2015/cyber_violence_gender%20report.pdf. Accessed on October 10, 2019.

Von Hentig, H. (1948). *The criminal and his victim: Studies in the socio-biology of crime*. New Haven, CT: Yale University Press.

Walby, S. (1989). Theorising patriarchy. *Sociology*, *23*(2), 213–234.

Walters, M., Wiedlitzka, S., Owusu-Bempah, A., & Goodall, K. (2017). *Hate crime and the legal process: Options for law reform*. Sussex: University of Sussex.

Weinstein, J. (1992). First amendment challengers to hate crime legislation: Where's the speech? *Criminal Justice Ethics*, *11*(2), 6–20.

Westbrook, L. (2008). Vulnerable subjecthood: The risks and benefits of the struggle for hate crime legislation. *Berkeley Journal of Sociology*, *52*, 3–23.

WHO. (2013). *Global and regional estimates of violence against women: Prevalence and health effects of intimate partner violence and non-partner sexual violence*. WHO, Department of Reproductive Health and Research, London School of Hygiene and Tropical Medicine, South African Medical Research Council. Retrieved from https://www.who.int/reproductivehealth/publications/violence/9789241564625/en/

Williams, M. (2006). *Virtually criminal: Crime, deviance and regulation online*. London: Routledge.

Williams, Z. (2018, April 25). 'Raw hatred': Why the 'incel' movement targets and terrorises women. *The Guardian*. Retrieved from https://www.theguardian.com/world/2018/apr/25/raw-hatred-why-incel-movement-targets-terrorises-women

Wolfgang, M. (1957). Victim precipitated criminal homicide. *Journal of Criminal Law, Criminology and Police Science*, *48*(1), 1–11.

Zempi, I., & Chakraborti, N. (2014). *Islamophobia, victimisation and the veil*. Basingstoke: Palgrave Macmillan.